Mac Perry's
FLORIDA LAWN
and GARDEN CARE

Mac Perry's

FLORIDA LAWN and GARDEN CARE

FLORIDA FLAIR BOOKS
Miami, Florida

Contents

Preface

Florida has become "pleasingly plump" with happy homeowners fleeing the chilly North – the homeland of yellow-gold forsythia, towering Norway spruce, and the dainty crocus that slivers its way through a late-fallen snow to greet the long-awaited spring.

But, in this fair land of sunshine, even the most polished gardener feels a bit tarnished when confronted by the glittering array of Florida plant and insect life.

The first question is usually, "What should I plant and where do I put it?" After acquiring the plants and digging the holes comes, "Will anything grow in this dirt?" After a few weeks we get, "When do I fertilize and with what?" In a few months it's "How do I prune this thing? It's getting bigger than the house!" Then ultimately comes the big one, "What are those little white things all over my plant; why are the leaves shriveling up?"

Do these questions sound a little too familiar? Well, don't feel lonely, I've talked to thousands with the same problems. Sometimes I've felt like a "Dear Abby" of the garden world.

To help you in your gardening, I have decided to jot down remedies for all the aches and pains your plants might get. Here they are along with hundreds of other hints on propagating, planting, pruning, choosing the right plant, and – well, just glance over the contents page and see for yourself.

I'd suggest you read one chapter a day, and at the end of each chapter review all previous chapters. In less than two weeks you'll know the tricks of the tropicals, and your tarnished ego will be glistening brightly again.

Good luck in your lawn and garden!

Mac Perry

Mac Perry's

**FLORIDA LAWN
and GARDEN CARE**

CHAPTER ONE
Bugs, Bugs, and More Bugs

Florida lawn and garden care might well begin with the elimination of that first big problem – bugs. But all problem-solving has a simple, systematic approach, and throughout this book I will tell you how to go about it.

Did You Know?

There are only three ways the plants in your yard can die. Just three things will get them when your back is turned. Sound simple? It is.

The first way I call "sneak attack." It works like this. While you're sitting-in-the-shade sipping lemonade (made from home-grown Florida lemons, of course), a tiny little bug sneaks up on your favorite posey and sinks his choppers into the tender new growth. Man, what a feast we have here. But the worst part is that he has brought along a few of his brothers and sisters. And after several hours of feasting, the fun begins – mating time. With total disregard to consanguinity, these lascivious varmints reproduce like it is the last thing they'll ever do (and for most it is). In the time it takes the neighborhood lawn man to groom your grounds, the bug population explodes a hundred-fold. Then look out when they start feeding! But there is a simple two-step remedy: (1) identify the culprit, and (2) blast him with the proper prescription. So let's take a stand right now and get to know these fifteen most wanted, notorious nuisances.

FIFTEEN INSECTS OF SHRUBS AND TREES

1. Scale: Many species of scale insects exist. Most are less than ¼-inch in size and have a crusty shell over their body. Scales may be found feeding on trunks, leaves, stems, or fruit. They are often mistaken for bumps and are ignored. Look for these insects on holly, camellia, citrus, aralia, pittosporum, sago palms, hibiscus, fig, peach, gardenia, avocado, ixora, rose, mango.

2. Aphids: Often called plant lice, the pear-shaped aphids are less than ¹⁄₁₆-inch long and usually white, tan, or green. They feed only on tender, new growth and thus are most common during spring when

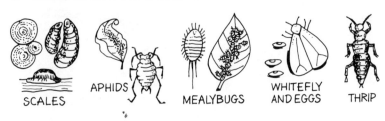

SCALES   APHIDS   MEALYBUGS   WHITEFLY AND EGGS   THRIP

growth is rapid. Look for aphids on leaves and stems of all house plants, citrus, viburnum, pittosporum, chrysanthemum, roses, and numerous other plants. Under a magnifying glass, the fat aphid is seen to have two small horns on his back side.

3. Mealybugs: A common insect, mealybugs feed on such plants as roses, azaleas, crotons, cacti, coleus, and almost all house plants. They are usually no more than ⅛-inch long, are yellowish-white, and oval in shape. Some have a long tail. Mealybugs are usually seen in cottony masses along leaf veins and where leaves are attached to the stem. These are sticky and contain eggs, tiny young, and mature mealybugs. Don't look for them where the sun is bright on the leaf. Actually, they prefer a little air conditioning.

4. White Fly: Another tiny pest, white flies usually feed on undersides of leaves of gardenia, ligustrum, viburnum, and especially citrus – plus a few other plants. The young emerge from flat, ¼-inch round, nearly translucent specks under the leaves. The adult is a tiny, heart-shaped, white fly that resembles a tiny snow flake in the air. Several of these insects will fly out of a disturbed limb. They appear from March through October.

5. Thrips: These small, slender insects are usually cream-colored or a deep, rich blue. Shed skins are seen as flakes of dust on curled leaves. Many feed on leaves, especially Cuban laurel, causing them to curl. Others feed on flowers. During the spring they produce their heaviest population, but they are also abundant throughout the warmer months.

It's Easy When You See It This Way

Insect pests are usually grouped into classes depending upon their feeding technique. The above listed insects are called *piercing-sucking* because they have mouthparts like a pointed straw that pierce the plant tissue and suck the juice out. The best and safest control is malathion or diazinon. Systemic controls may be used on house plants but should never be used on edible plants. These chemicals enter the plant's vein system, making the sap poisonous to the sucking insect.

Insects in the group below have *chewing* mouthparts. They chew plant parts and differ from sucking insects in several ways. Often it is not necessary to see or identify a chewing insect as control for most of them is the same. Simply look for the symptoms of chewed plant leaves or stems. About the safest control today is Sevin (carbaryl). Dust or spray, whichever method you prefer.

6. Caterpillars: Caterpillars are larvae that later as pupae form cocoons and turn into adult moths or butterflies. These adults mate, lay eggs, and die. Thus, the life cycle continues. Many species feed on landscape plants causing holes and irregular areas to appear in leaves. Others eat the entire leaf. Positive identification is *not* necessary. Dust or spray Sevin following label directions.

Occasionally, a large caterpillar, such as the horn worm, will appear. These are too large to be affected by the chemical. In this case the old A-B method of control is needed. Acquire two bricks; mark one A, the other B. Place the large insect on brick A, then simply slam A and B together. It works every time, even on those hard-to-kill bugs.

7. Beetles: Some beetles like leaves, others prefer flowers. Some eat during the day, others at night. All are hard-shelled insects, and most have larvae (the young worms) that feed on roots or bore through stems and branches. Besides Sevin, diazinon is an effective, safe control.

8. Grasshoppers and Katydids: These rather large insect pests consume abundant quantities of foliage, often stripping a plant completely. Grasshoppers are easy to see, but katydids are green and feed at night, making them more difficult to discover. Because of their size the A-B method of control is suggested. Sevin has been helpful.

9. Cutworms: Many harmless moths are cutworms before their methamorphosis. Usually they stay in the soil during the day and feed on tender young plants at night, cutting them off just above the ground. Some cutworms climb up the plant and feed on buds and leaves. Bait tossed on the ground in the late afternoon usually provides an effective control. Ask for cutworm bait at your local garden supply store.

10. Bagworms: These small worms spin a silken sac around themselves and attach bits of leaves and twigs to their bag as they feed. These

KATYDID

CUTWORM

BAGWORM

bags hang from plants, and the worms stick their heads out to feed. Bags may be up to two inches long. Best control is to pick off the bags and throw them in the garbage. Sevin has proved an effective spray when applied before the bag is formed.

Learn to Recognize the Group

Notice the main difference between the suckers and chewers in the Insect Comparison Chart. Remember, it is usually unnecessary to name the insect in order to determine what control measure to take. From the symptoms, simply determine to which group the culprit belongs and choose the appropriate control.

There are other insects that have rasping mouthparts and lapping mouthparts such as flies that regurgitate on their food to dissolve it, and then lap it up. But these are usually unimportant to the home gardener.

The pests listed 11 through 15 stand separate from the suckers and chewers but should be given careful study because of their abundance in the garden.

Insect Comparison Chart

	Sucking Insects	Chewing Insects
Size	tiny, usually less than ¼ inch	large, one to two inches
Mobility	usually don't move more than a few inches in lifetime	may move from plant to plant or yard to yard
Where They Feed	usually on undersides of leaves or stems in shade	all over the plant especially the leaves
Population	several are necessary to cause plant damage	one or two may cause severe damage
Symptoms	weak or no growth cottony masses or sticky leaves*	chewed leaves or stems
Best Control	Malathion	Sevin

*Note: Sucking insects excrete a sweet syrup called honey dew. As this falls to the upper surface of lower leaves a black fungus called sooty mold begins to cover the leaves. Volck oil spray will cause the soot to flake off. Ants have been known to protect aphid eggs through a cold winter, delivering them up to tender new leaves in spring until they begin feeding. They then tickle their ribs to milk the sweet honey dew from them. This procedure is reminiscent of man's practice with cows.

11. Leaf Miners: These are tiny insects that come from a small fly which deposits her eggs between the upper and lower surface of leaves. From the egg hatches a maggot that mines his way through the leaf, cutting veins supplying the outer part of the leaf. The miner leaves a white, serpentine line to reveal his path. It harms tomatoes and many annuals as well as azalea, holly, and several other plants. Control by spraying diazinon.

12. Spider Mites: Also called red spiders, spider mites are one of the most common pests of Florida plants during hot, dry periods. Their size makes them nearly invisible to the naked eye. Look for shed skins under leaves of weak plants. These skins are often so numerous that they cause the leaf to appear dusty or sandy. Look for them especially on crotons growing in the shade. Mites are easily seen with a 10-power magnifying glass, which can be obtained at biological supply stores for a few dollars. Control spider mites with Kelthane.

13. Psocids: An ever-increasing insect are the psocids (so´-sids) or algae cows, so called because they feed on the algae growing on tree trunks during humid, damp weather. You'll first notice a silk web closely hugging the tree trunk spun by the psocids for protection. These insects cause no harm to the tree and can usually be washed away with a strong spray from the garden hose if webs become unsightly. The tiny insects may occasionally be seen massed in a herd. Wave your hand and they all scatter in the same direction like cattle.

14. Bark Beetles: Several bark beetles attack trees in Florida – especially pines and oaks. Usually, tiny shot holes can be seen in the bark. If trees are kept healthy they will resist the beetles by pushing them out with sap. Look for these sap tubes. Otherwise, squirt a mixture of half lindane and half water in each tiny hole and seal it up with putty. Lindane, mixed at the label rate, should then be sprayed over the lower ten feet of bark on the trunk.

15. Slugs and Snails: These slow movers are not insects but are injurious to plants in damp, shady locations. They feed at night, devouring foliage. Slugs look like snails without shells. Recommended control is metaldehyde.

LEAF MINER
DAMAGE

SPIDER MITE

PSOCID
WEB

BARK
BEETLE
DAMAGE

Are Pesticides Harmful?

Many homeowners are concerned (as they should be) about pesticides polluting the environment. Florida, however, has very good laws regulating the sale of harmful chemicals. In general, any chemical sold legally over the counter is environmentally safe when used according to the label-recommended rate. Chemicals that should be used sparingly, if not used carefully, may harm pets, birds, or people. Other chemicals mentioned in this book, especially malathion, Sevin, Kelthane, and diazinon, are relatively safe to the environment. Regardless of what chemical is used, it is a good idea to keep small pets away from sprayed areas for at least twenty-four hours.

1. Never spray or dust on windy days.
2. Wash face, arms, and hands with lots of soap after each use.
3. Never spray around dog's dish, bird bath, fish pond, etc.
4. After each use, pour out unused portion of mixed spray. It will not keep more than a few days.
5. Always leave chemicals in their original containers with labels intact. You never know when you'll need the chemical name or its antidote for a physician.
6. Always keep chemicals locked up out of reach of children and pets.

Just How Many Bugs Are There?

Before you get "bugged" from reading about all these insects, let me explain that not all insects are harmful. As a matter of fact only about one percent of all identified insects are called pests because of the harm they cause to plants, man, and animals. This one percent, however, costs the United States over three billion dollars annually.

As a point of interest, it should be noted that of all the thousands of species of insects inhabiting the earth, over seventy-five percent have not even been studied and named. And since many useful products are derived from insects, ecologists object to the disruption of unstudied natural systems in isolated areas like the Everglades.

Insects are man's greatest competitors on earth Approximately eighty percent of all the animals in the world belong to the class *Insecta*. They have such a tremendous ability to reproduce that if two flies mate in April and all of their progeny live to maturity, reproducing at the normal rate, five months later they would cover the earth four feet deep. Several female insects (aphids and mites come to mind) can reproduce without a male being around.

Now—Go Get 'em!

You have studied identification and control of fifteen of the most popular insects of Florida gardens. I have not mentioned lawn pests, for these will be discussed in a later chapter. Insects are the first cause of plant ailments to suspect when trouble-shooting plant problems. The other two causes will be outlined in the next chapter. For now, take the rest of the week to search your yard, shrubs, trees, and other plants. See how many "buggers" you can find and identify. Remember, many insects are abundant only during certain seasons. So in sixty days there may be a whole new group of pests chopping away at your plants. Check on them periodically. The important thing to remember is that you rarely have to identify the insect—simply determine if it has chewing or sucking mouthparts as outlined in the comparison chart. Then spray Sevin or malathion. If in doubt, mix the two together and spray. Didn't I tell you it would be simple?

CHAPTER TWO
Why Plants Die

As stated in chapter one, there are only three ways your plants can die. In analyzing plant problems, first suspect insects because they are the easiest to diagnose. If an insect has not caused your flowery friend to fade, then look for what I call "sneakier attack." This devastation occurs when another creature – one very similar to the insect in that it comes to life, feeds, grows, reproduces, and dies, leaving a host of offspring – hits the bushes. The big difference in this second devastator is the size. To the naked eye he is invisible. Horticulturists call them pathogens, you may know them as germs. Actually, there are four pathogens and because of their persistence in the Florida environment they demand respect. They are Mr. Fungus, Mr. Virus, Mr. Bacterium, and Mr. Nematode. It is rare that a plant pathogen will ever attack the gardener. It prefers the plant.

These tiny organisms rob the host plant by clogging and damaging the vital organs (such as the plant's vein system), preventing their proper function. Thus the plant takes on a sad appearance that we call diseased. It may die from the disease. So let us take a stand right now and learn these symptoms of diseases that give us a pain in the green thumb.

LEARN THESE FIFTEEN DISEASE SYMPTOMS

1. Leaf Spots: These, the most common of all diseases, are irregular areas in the leaves, often with concentric halos around the spot. Rain or watering plant leaves often spreads the disease. Black spot on roses is a good example in Florida. Collect and burn infected leaves. Spray benomyl, zineb, maneb, or neutral copper.

2. Mildew: Whitish powder may appear on leaves or stem, especially on crape myrtle and roses, causing the leaves to yellow and die. Common during seasons of cool nights and warm days and particularly in shady, damp locations. Avoid crowding plants and spray weekly with benomyl, Daconil 2787, or folpet until disease gives up.

3. Mosaic: Caused by an extremely small virus pathogen, mosaics usually appear as lined patterns across a leaf, but may be circular. This disease is spread by aphids and by propagating from a diseased plant.

18

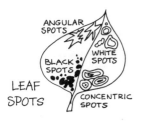

Chemical control is often not helpful. Destroy all diseased plants, keep down weeds that may carry the virus, and spray malathion to control aphids.

4. Damp Off: Commonly attacks young seedling annuals, such as petunia and tomato. The fungus strikes the stem base at ground level, causing it to turn brown, shrivel, and topple to its death. Destroy diseased plants and sterilize soil with Vapam. This chemical must not be used near roots of healthy plants. If propagating from seed, use shredded sphagnum moss as a medium. Drench young plants with Fermate before disease spreads.

5. Wilt: Often caused by bacteria, wilts cause leaves and stem to droop and appear water-soaked. Later, leaves shrivel and dry out. A cut stem may ooze yellow or brown water-soaked material. Symptoms usually begin on lower leaves and seem to be more common on the succulent tropicals, annuals, and vegetables. Collect and burn diseased plants; replace with varieties resistant to wilt. Take cuttings from healthy plants and place potted plants in a warmer location. Chemical control is not practical.

6. Cankers: Symptoms frequently appear on stems or canes of plants. Areas may be speckled, blotched, or even scabby. Often they are sunken and sometimes crack open. If canker enlarges around the stem, it will strangle growth beyond the diseased area causing die-back, an advanced symptom. Carefully prune a few inches below cankers and burn cuttings.

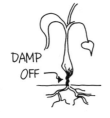

7. Gall: Enlarged areas around stems and base of trunk could be galls caused by bacteria entering exposed wounds, especially around a grafted trunk. Galls may become quite large. Other galls are caused by fungi or insects. Remove smaller plants and sterilize soil with Vapam before replanting. Larger plants must have galls cut out by a reputable tree surgeon. Often, galls appear as marble-size swellings on leaves of oaks. These cause little damage. Drench soil with diazinon to control root chewers wounding plants.

8. Scab: Often appears as rough, crusty areas on stems, leaves, fruit or roots. Common on poinsettia. Leaves usually wither and die early. Best control is to prune out diseased parts and spray remainder with captan or sulfur.

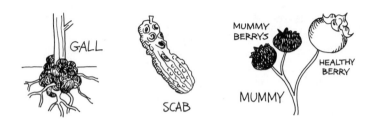

9. Mummy: Mummified fruits appear on some trees in wet, humid areas. The ends of new shoots usually wilt and turn brown, leaving the fruit in a dark, shriveled condition. Fruit becomes hard. Avoid crowding plants and do not overfertilize. Apply captan or zineb weekly.

10. Fruit Rot: Other fruit diseases include rotting. Affected areas are usually rounded and may run together. This disease frequently starts at the blossom end of the fruit opposite the stem end. Mulch vegetables to keep fruit from contacting the moist soil. Spray malathion and Sevin to control disease-carrying insects. Don't drop or wound fruit. Dust or spray with an all-purpose fungicide like zineb or maneb.

11. Petal Blight: Azaleas are prone to this disease during wet seasons. As flowers form, small specks appear under flower petals. In about twenty-four hours, flowers become soggy and limp. As flowers rot, they become covered with a white mold and cling to leaves or stem. Pick off diseased flowers as soon as you see them. Spray lightly with zineb, Daconil 2787, or maneb every other day during blooming season.

12. Butt Rot: Fungi may enter drought cracks of certain palms or other trees causing an infection that later produces a shell-like conk

FRUIT ROT

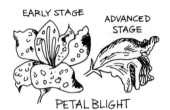

EARLY STAGE

ADVANCED STAGE

PETAL BLIGHT

BUTT ROT

protruding from the trunk near the base or butt. One of these conks has the capacity to shed over 100 billion spores in a single day, occcasionally causing toadstools to appear around the base of the tree. Paint exposed wounds with pruning paint. If rot appears, cut out damaged wood and paint all exposed wood with a solution of one part household bleach to five parts of water for sterilization prior to applying pruning paint.

13. Bulb Rot: Bulbs, corms, and rhizomes may also become diseased. Shoots may appear weak and die back, starting at the tip, or may not emerge at all. Upon examination, roots are decayed and spots of rot appear on side of bulb. These bulbs are usually lightweight and spongy. Disease spreads when bulbs are stored in hot, moist locations. After digging bulbs, dry them thoroughly and rapidly. Dust bulbs with captan.

14. Root Rot: Affected plants lose vigor either rapidly or slowly. Often the entire plant droops. Water and fertilizer rarely seem to help. The younger the plant, the more rapidly it wilts and dies. Roots decay and may be mushy or firm. Nematodes often cause the wound through which the fungi or bacteria enter. Root rot is more common on annual flowers in cool, poorly drained areas. Drench soil of suspect plants with Terraclor. Dig up and burn infected plants. Sterilize soil with Vapam before replanting. Avoid overwatering.

15. Nematodes: Perhaps the most notorious of parasites, several nematodes feed on and in the roots of almost all plants and grasses. One species, rootknot, can be detected by simply examining the roots for

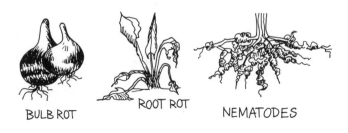

BULB ROT

ROOT ROT

NEMATODES

galls. A soil test, available at your County Extension office, will ascertain the extent of infestation from other species. Your first suspicion should come when a plant fails to grow after two years. It just sits there staring at you with that "I'm-not-budging" look on its face. Plants may appear unhealthy and weak. They often shed their leaves prematurely or produce small fruit or leaves on broadleaf evergreens. Death may occur over a period of several months. Plants usually respond temporarily to water and fertilizer. If you suspect this microscopic worm is feeding on the roots of plants showing a slow decline in health, have soil treated by a certified pest control-operator using Mo-Cap, a restricted chemical.

HOW TO PREVENT SPREAD OF DISEASE

In disease control, preventive measures are always better than curative ones. Here are sixteen ways you can prevent diseases in your yard.

1. Always burn diseased plants, never put them in a compost pile or use as mulch.

2. Control weeds in and around plant beds.

3. Rotate annual plants from year to year, never plant the same plant in the same spot in consecutive years.

4. Always buy Florida-developed varieties of plants when they are available. These are usually more disease-resistant than northern varieties.

5. Use only certified seed or transplants when available.

6. When collecting your own seed or bulbs, dust them with captan or thiram after they dry.

7. Never water *tops* of plants unless they are dusty or infested with spider mites, and then only during late morning hours and on non-diseased plants.

8. Dip pruning equipment occasionally in 40% formaldehyde (Formalin) or rubbing alcohol to destroy any disease pathogens that might be on the blades from pruning a diseased plant.

9. Always practice good sanitation in garden work areas, such as hanging hose nozzles on a hook when not in use.

10. Wash hands thoroughly after handling a diseased plant.

11. Spray plants periodically with an all-purpose fungicide such as liquid copper to prevent diseases from entering.

12. Spray often to control insects that may spread diseases. Use a safe, mild insecticide such as diazinon, malathion, and Sevin.

13. When spraying always use the correct chemical, at the rate shown on the label, and get good coverage over entire plant.

14. Heavy rains may spread diseases. This is difficult to combat. Expensive specimen plants may be covered by building a small, temporary, polyethylene greenhouse over plant.

15. For potted plants use only sterile soil. You can sterilize your own soil by placing a damp mixture two inches thick on a cookie sheet and heat in an oven at 200° for forty-five minutes.

16. After removing a diseased plant, always treat soil with Vapam before replanting. Remember to never drench Vapam around the roots of healthy plants, it will kill them. Replanting can be done two to three weeks after treatment.

A SIMPLE WAY TO SPRAY!

Often the question is asked, "Can I mix my insecticides and fungicides in the same sprayer and spray just once?" Usually, the answer is yes. Most pesticides are compatible. For years I have mixed malathion (for piercing sucking insects), Sevin (for the chewers), and liquid copper (an all-purpose fungicide for diseases). This solution is sprayed on most all my plants March 1, April 1, August 1, and September 1. This is purely a preventive procedure. If an insect or disease dares to show itself during the interim, he is immediately identified and curative control measures are taken. When mixing chemicals, mix at the label rate, adding each chemical to the same gallon of water.

One word of caution. Herbicides (weed killers) should always be used in a sprayer separate from other pesticides because many are very difficult to wash out, and plant damage may occur. This means you will need two sprayers. The inexpensive, all plastic, trigger sprayers are excellent for small jobs. Hose-end sprayers are good for the bigger jobs such as lawn, grove, or hedge spraying.

HOW TO ANALYZE PLANT PROBLEMS

Here is a unique, simple, and systematic approach to diagnosing plant problems. When you first become suspicious that death to your darling is imminent, then begin your analysis this way:

1. Insects: Consider first if the condition might be caused by an insect (sneak attack) by doing the following:

a) Suckers: Look for evidence of black soot on leaves or stem. Look for tiny insects on underside of young leaves or stems. They are usually found in large numbers. Small, flakey, shed skins may be seen under leaves. Plant parts may be sticky. If any of these symptoms are noticed spray malathion or one of the other recommendations.

b) Chewers: After eliminating suckers as possible cause of the problem, look closely for any larger beetles or caterpillars. There may be only one or two of these. Look especially for chewed leaves or stems. Dust or spray Sevin if symptoms are found.

c) Miscellaneous: If suckers or chewers are not the problem, check for mites by rubbing the underside of a suspect leaf across a sheet of white paper and look for blood streaks. Mites are usually not seen with the naked eye but leaf may appear sandy or speckled. Spray Kelthane if mites are found. Check for white lines in leaf, indicating leaf miner. Be observant to any other possible insect pest. After making this analysis, and if the diagnosis is not yet known, continue on with the next category (sneakier attack).

2. Disease: Most often the symptoms of a disease will manifest themselves in the form of leaf spots, wilt, rot, blight, or one of the other mentioned conditions. In many cases the plant simply looks weak or sick, especially if it has a root disease. If the specific disease cannot be determined, then spray entire plant and drench soil around roots with neutral copper, Dithane M-45, or some other broad-spectrum fungicide. If plant is slowly dying over a long period of time, and especially if it perks up temporarily after watering, then you might suspect nematodes.

3. Other: If, after investigating the above possibilities, you find no solution to your plant's problem, then it is time to suspect the third cause of plant death. This I call "sneakiest attack" because, it is the most difficult to diagnose. In this case, some physical or environmental action is interferring with your plant's normal way of life. Here I've listed a few possibilities. Most of these will be developed more thoroughly in chapter three.

a) Drought: A lack of rain or watering will cause plants to wilt and lose their glossy sheen.

b) Wet Feet: First sign is yellow veins in leaves. Then leaves turn brown but do not fall for several days.

c) Fertilizer Burn: Usually appears as a leaf margin or tip burn. Water plants extra heavily daily to flush out fertilizer.

d) Nutrient Deficiency: Often appears as a loss of green color in areas between veins. Fertilize with a complete fertilizer.

e) Light: Indoor plants will grow tall and spindly in a light-deficient situation. Excess sunlight causes leaf burn on that part of the leaf closest to the sun (usually the middle of the leaf where it bends).

f) Dog Damage: Male dogs have been known to cause a burn to one side of a shrub. They prefer to come to the same shrub daily. Try using a dog repellent available at pet stores.

g) Salt Burn: Beach dwellers must use salt-resistant plants. Salt will travel in the evening mist causing damage to plants many blocks inland. See chapter four for a list of salt-tolerant plants.

h) Builders Disease: This covers a multitude of possibilities, especially around a new home. Boards or concrete may be buried beneath the plant, preventing root penetration. Plaster, cement, or chemicals poured or buried in the soil might cause a pH problem (have your soil tested). Raised plant beds may have no drainage.

i) Weather: Excess cold, frost, heat, or humidity will destroy many plants not native to your area. The majority of northern plants simply will not grow in Florida.

j) Planted Too Deep: Leaves turn brown and usually hang on plant several weeks. Raise plant up several inches. Especially common on azaleas.

You see – just three things can kill your plants: insects, disease, environmental interference. Now that you know what it takes to kill plants, we'll talk about what it takes to keep them alive. The above three things must be kept away from your plants, but there are four things your plants must receive, and in the right quantity. These are explained in the next chapter.

CHAPTER THREE

How to Keep Your Plants Healthy

Did you know that Mother Nature is actually working against you by hindering your plant's growth? "How is this?" you say. "Mother Nature gave us these plants and they grew under the natural laws of the earth." Well, not exactly. Over the centuries man, through genetics and plant breeding, has brought about more lush, leafy plants with larger, brighter flowers. These are actually freaks of a more stable variety, and if left alone would, according to Mendel's law of degeneration, revert back to the wilder variety. That is why plant culture has reached the magnitude it has today. All of our plants have an ancestor that is stronger but not as colorful. So, odd as it may seem, we must actually supervise our plants to see that Mother Nature does not give too much or too little of the four ingredients of life: Light, Heat, Water, and Fertilizer.

LIGHT

Light supplies the energy for plants to grow. Through a mysterious process called photosynthesis, plants absorb water from the soil and carbon dioxide from the air and convert them to simple sugars and energy containing compounds that we call food. In order for this food-producing process to take place, energy is needed. This energy comes from light.

Light Has Three Characteristics

1. Light Intensity: This characteristic refers to the actual brightness of the light. Full sun in Florida produces about 12,000 foot-candles (ft-c) of light, while a cloudy day or shaded sun will produce only about 3,000 ft-c. In the average home on a bright day, house plants growing in dark areas of the home, such as a bathroom where only artificial light is supplied, will receive an intensity less than 30 ft-c.

Notice the great difference of intensity in the following four locations.

12,000 ft-c—full sun
3,000 ft-c—full shade
300 ft-c—living room
30 ft-c—bathroom

Most people are not aware that walking from a typical bathroom to the outdoors results in a light intensity increase of 40,000%. The reason is simple. We have pupils in our eyes that automatically adjust to every light intensity so that we do not notice the change as much. Plants do not have pupils and feel the full impact of the change. The reason why I mention all this is very important:

a) Sun-loving plants, including most evergreens, flowering plants, annuals, and vegetables must be planted where they will receive 5,000 to 12,000 ft-c of light intensity daily. This explains why roses do poorly in the shade.

b) Shade-loving plants will get leaf burn if planted in full sun, or slowly die if planted indoors. They prefer an intensity of 500 to 5,000 ft-c.

c) Indoor plants prefer an intensity between 50 and 500 ft-c and will surely burn up if you plunge them in the full sun for a "sun bath" boost. Many have tried this and lost their prize "pets." Become acquainted with the light intensity requirements of your plants and place them in a location receiving that amount. Never, never give a plant a "sun bath." Plants slowly adapt to their environment and if moved to an extreme environment will go into shock. A small foot-candle light meter will prove beneficial if you like to grow house plants. Or use your camera lightmeter.

As you get to know new plants, try to get a feel for their light requirements. Here is a partial list to help you get started:

Plants Preferring 5,000 - 12,00 ft-c (Full Sun)	Plants Preferring 500 - 5,000 ft-c (Shade/Florida Room)	Plants Preferring 50 - 500 ft-c (Living Room)
Most Palms	Large Leaf Philo-dendrons	Syngonium
Most Shade Trees	Azaleas	Pepperomia
Most Evergreens	Pittosporum	Chinese Evergreen
Cacti	Caladium	Several Ficus Trees
Most Fruit Trees	Bromelaids	Most Philodendron
Hibiscus	Orchids	Hoya
Roses	Most Ground Covers	Sansevieria
Powderpuff	Dracena	Begonia
Plumbago	Jacobinia	African Violet
Jasmine	Most Tropicals	Gloxinia
Annuals		Most House Plants

2. Light Duration: The second characteristic of light refers to the number of hours the plant receives light. Not how strong, but *how long.* Most full-sun plants, that is those preferring 5,000 to 12,000 ft-c, like to be in contact with this amount of light for at least six hours. For shade lovers, duration is not critical. For house plants receiving a minimum amount of light, say 50 ft-c, leave lights on for 14 hours. In other words, if you have plants growing in your bathroom you had better leave a light on all night. The lower the light intensity, the longer the duration is needed.

Light duration is also important to plants that are "day sensitive." "Short day" plants such as poinsettia, Christmas cactus, and chrysanthemum require about twelve hours of uninterrupted darkness before they set flower buds. That is why they bloom in late fall. If a poinsettia is planted under a street light, it will never receive the required twelve hours of darkness and may never bloom. If Christmas cactus is kept in a pot in a living room that is lighted at night, it too may never bloom.

Summer-flowering plants such as shasta daisy are called "long day" plants and will not set flowers until they receive about fourteen hours of light per day.

By artificially controlling the light duration on certain plants (Easter lily, Christmas cactus, poinsettia, mums), greenhouse growers can control the exact day their potted plants will be ready for the market. This is important for holiday plants. It also allows the grower to produce mums on a year-round basis, covering them with a black cloth at 5 p.m. in summer, and lighting them during the long winter nights. It fools the plant. This discovery about light duration affecting the setting of flower buds is called photoperiodism.

3. Light Quality: The third characteristic of light refers to the wave length of the light rays. Not how strong or how long but *how good.* One end of the light spectrum is red, the other blue. The extreme ends of the spectrum are called infrared and ultraviolet. The sun provides the full spectrum, and plants just love it. Light quality becomes important when artificial light is used to supply energy for house plants.

When you get a chance, notice that an incandescent light bulb gives off a reddish tint while a flourescent tube gives off a bluish tint. Perhaps you've bought clothes at a store that appeared one color (under the store's flourescent lights) but when you brought them home (under your incandescent bulbs) they seemed to have changed color.

In general, flourescent tubes will give off a brighter, more intense light, but the plants do not seem to respond as well to blue light as they do the red. Actually, it is good to grow house plants under both –

flourescent tubes provide the required intensity and incandescent bulbs provide the more desired quality.

Manufacturers have developed a flourescent bulb that will provide both of these characteristics and is ideal for growing and propagating plants indoors. These bulbs are sold under the name Grow Lux.

In summary, you should become aware of all your plant's light needs or at least develop a feel for their requirements. Be conscious of the light *intensity* (how strong), *duration* (how long), and *quality* (how good) being supplied to your plants.

I have found that it is intensity that causes the majority of the light problems. Here are the symptoms to look for:

Too Much Light: Symptoms are often found on house plants and other potted plants that have been conditioned to shade, then plunged into the sun. On plants with long or large leaves, you will notice a sun scorch on that area of the leaf most exposed to the sun, usually at the center of the leaf. Backside and inner portions appear normal. Smaller-leafed plants and especially those with delicate, tender leaves will show a pale color, then the leaf tips, and the margins will turn brown. Newer leaves toward the top of the plant will wilt and die.

Too Little Light: Plants that prefer full sun are often potted and brought indoors where they are expected to live indefinitely. This is all right for a weekend, but plants should be quickly returned to a brighter location. All too common is the juniper bonsai plant that is placed on the living room coffee table (a low light area). These plants can be expected to live about thirty days if you're lucky. Most evergreens show the symptoms when it is too late to do anything about it. The more succulent, leafy plants will develop long, spindly shoots with small leaves. The internode area between the leaves will be elongate.

Look again at the light-intensity list. It is usually the full-sun group suffering from a light deficiency or the house-plant group suffering form excess light that causes most of the problems. In either case, the plant will go into shock and should be moved to a recuperating area like the Florida room or a shaded porch before returning it to its desired location.

HEAT

Every plant has a temperature range in which it enjoys maximum growth. As the temperature drops below this range, growth slows or ceases, causing eventual death. As the temperature rises above this range, stored food reserves within the plant are used up and the plant simply grows itself to death.

Heat requirements of plants should be studied so that you will know why northern plants do not grow in Florida and why South Florida plants do not grow in North Florida.

Why Do Northern Plants Die in Florida?

It is now understood that northern plants brought to Florida actually grow themselves to death. Why? Because food production (photosynthesis) remains about the same as there is little difference in the light intensities of north and south. But because Florida has higher year-round temperatures, food digestion (respiration) increases. And if food digestion becomes greater than food production, the plant will shrivel and die. It will use up all the stored foods – grow itself to death.

The above process occurs on such plants as northern apples, pears, rhubarb, aspargus, snapdragon, larkspur, violets, spruce, hemlock, hens, chicks, and many others.

Another important reason why northern plants, especially deciduous shrubs and trees such as walnut, hickory, and forsythia, do poorly in warmer parts of Florida has to do with dormancy. These plants go into dormancy, a rest period, in the early fall after a season of vigorous growth. They simply get tired and fall asleep. It is the cold, northern winters that shock these plants out of dormancy, waking them up to bloom and leaf out in the spring. In Florida, the temperature may not get low enough to cause this shock. And as spring rolls around the plants are still half asleep. They slowly die after a couple of years.

Northern bulbs like tulip, daffodil, and crocus must be dug up in the fall, refrigerated during the winter, and replanted in January to simulate the shock period. I have found that 40 days of 40 degrees is sufficient to break the dormancy of most bulbs.

Why South Florida Plants Die in North Florida

Just as excess heat causes complications in plant growth, so does excess cold. South Florida plants grown in North Florida suffer from three possible cold damages:

1. Freeze: Moisture in the unprotected, fleshy leaves, stems, or trunks of many tropicals will freeze, expand, and split the plant tissue causing cells to break down with the result of plant injury or death.

2. Frost: Where frost comes into contact with plant leaves, a chemical burning occurs that destroys plant tissue. To protect plants from frost or freeze, cover them with burlap, pasteboard boxes, or some other insulating material (never use plastic). Light bulbs can be burned beneath this cover to add heat to the plant's environment during extra-cold nights.

3. Cold Wind: Some plants will survive a mild freeze and frost, but will suffer from cold wind. Crotons, for example, drop their leaves if exposed to cold wind.

In Florida there is only a mild winter and plants never go into complete dormancy. As Florida plants remain in a growing state, they tend to produce tender new shoots and leaves. It is this new growth that frequently gets winter-burned on the few cold nights we have.

The symptoms of cold damage are usually a browning of the leaf margins, especially on newer growth, and leaf drop. Damage may be most severe on the side of the plant exposed to the cold winds.

WATER

Water has several purposes in plants. We have already seen that it is part of the photosynthetic reaction and, therefore, necessary for plant growth.

It also serves as a solvent for dry fertilizers, allowing them to enter the plant's root system. In this case, a water deficiency means the fertilizer elements go back into the dry form and possibly burn the plant roots. This malady, called fertilizer burn, is caused as much by water deficiency as by excess fertilizer.

Water also serves as the vehicle for hormones, vitamins, and various plant foods inside the plant. The moisture carries these elements to where they are needed within the plant.

It has been seen that CO_2 is needed for food production and ultimate plant growth. CO_2 is a gas which enters the plant through tiny pores called stomates. These pores are held open by guard cells swollen with water. If plants are not watered, these cells go flaccid and lose their turgor pressure causing the pores to close. The CO_2 cannot enter the plant, and photosynthesis is stopped. If plants are not watered soon, permanent damage and ultimate death occur.

As CO_2 enters these pores, moisture leaves through the same opening. This water loss is normal and is called transpiration. An increase in temperature or wind, or a decrease in relative humidity causes transpiration or water loss, to increase. If the amount of water leaving the plant is greater than the amount entering through the roots, wilt again occurs. I see much of this during the winter months when plants are seldom watered. Wilting is actually a self-preservation mechanism that allows the plant to retain its moisture by stopping transpiration. But, we can also see that it stops food production by preventing the entry of CO_2.

Too Little Water

All plants can stand some wilting for a given length of time before permanent damage occurs. Some plants, such as wedelia, will wilt badly and show shriveling, drying leaves, but when watered will freshen back to normal within the hour if the permanent wilting point (PWP) was not reached. If watering is delayed a couple of days, only a portion of the plant will recover, leaving the new leaves permanently damaged. In this case it is said that the permanent wilting point had been reached. Try to become familiar with the permanent wilting point of your plants.

Some plants, especially those adapted to more arid regions such as cacti and succulents, will go for weeks without water. But the tropical rain forest plants like philodendron prefer to be watered more often.

Too Much Water

Another important factor concerning water is called wet feet. During the rainy season in Florida (mid-summer to fall in North and Central Florida; April through November in South Florida), abundant water floods the ground causing the water table to come up into the root zone of deep-rooted trees, thus weakening them. As the rain enters the surface, the water table rises and oxygen is pushed out of the soil causing what is known as wet feet. Roots rot and plant begins to show damage.

The symptoms of wet feet are browning and drooping leaves, especially on newer growth. These leaves usually remain on the plant a few days before falling.

I have noticed that wet feet occurs readily on *Ligustrum lucidum, podocarpus,* and citrus trees.

When watering, it is best to water less frequently and use more water. Frequent shallow watering encourages roots to remain near the surface where there is moisture. This can be dangerous during seasons of drought or water bans when the roots are left to the mercy of the scorching sun.

Water your plants thoroughly twice a week for best results. Plants requiring more moisture can be planted with 50% peat moss and mulched heavily and still receive the same two waterings a week.

With house plants and hanging baskets provide drainage holes for excess moisture. The best solution is to leave the plant in its original nursery container and place this inside a larger, more decorative pot. After you water, excess water can be poured from the decorative pot. It usually doesn't hurt to leave an inch or two of water in the bottom of this pot.

FERTILIZER

The fourth and final ingredient for plants to live is fertilizer. This is such an important topic that I have devoted an entire chapter to it later. Fertilizer elements, in one form or another, are absolutely essential for plant growth. Over-fertilizing, however, results in foliage turning brown or black, leaf tips showing burn, and possibly rapid death. If you suspect plants to be over-fertilized, flood the ground twice a day for a few days to leach out excess fertilizer. Under-fertilizing results in stunting and poor growth. Plants then become weak and susceptible to disease attack.

The solution to "how to keep your plants healthy" can now be summarized by saying they must be placed in an environment whereby they receive optimum and desired quantities of light, heat, water, and fertilizer. An excess or deficiency of one or more of these essentials of life will cause plant problems.

You have noticed by now that these four ingredients overlap the subject of chapter two called "sneakiest attack." You are so right. The real secret to making plants live is the elimination of 1.) insects, 2.) disease, and 3.) excess or deficient environmental elements in your plant's life.

But, let's not linger here, there is a whole new world ahead of us in identifying plants in the landscape and knowing what plant to use in that special location.

CHAPTER FOUR

Know Your Plants by Name

Ever wonder where those long, fancy plant names came from? In this chapter I will explain this as well as describe over one hundred different landscape plants, many of which you may already be growing. These plants are all common, so visit a few nurseries and learn to identify them.

HOW PLANTS GET THEIR NAMES

Many years ago as plants gained popularity in certain regions of the world they were given localized names. Soon it was discovered that the same plant had been given many names. Much confusion arose from this method so it was mutually decided that plants should be described and given one name that would be recognized by everyone.

The language chosen was Latin since it was recognized by most leading nations. The man who led the team for plant classification was a Swedish botanist named Linnaeus who lived in the 1700s.

All living matter was divided into two *kingdoms;* the plant kingdom, if the matter had cell walls containing cellulose, and the animal kingdom if it did not.

When looking at all the plant kingdom, groups were seen that had similar characteristics. These groups were called *phyla* or *branches.*

The branches were further divided into *classes* and each class divided into several *orders.*

Within each order of plants there exists several *families.* Perhaps you have used the term "plant family" before.

Each family is divided into *genera* (singular: genus). And each genus is divided into *species.*

By this method, all living matter could be grouped into its own kingdom, phylum, class, order, family, genus, and species.

If anyone asks for the scientific (botanical) name or Latin binomial of a plant, they are asking for the genus and species. Look for these names in books and on signs at the botanical garden. The genus is always given first and is capitalized, while the species is in lower case. Both are usually underlined or written in italics.

Scientific Names Are Interesting

Let's look at an example. All roses belong to the genus *Rosa*. To further describe each rose, the species name is attached. The *Rosa alba* is the white rose; *Rosa sinensis,* the Chinese rose; and *Rosa lancifolia,* a rose with lance-shaped foliage.

Plant geneticists have hybridized many plants producing new plants that are improvements on the old species. Rather than make new species out of these they are simply called *varieties* of the species. Often the varietal name is taken from that of the hybridizer, or one of his family or loved ones. Thus we have *Ilex cornuta burfordi,* an improved variety of the Chinese holly, which was introduced by a man named Burford. When you see three names on a sign at the park they are genus, species, and variety. Look to see if the variety and species tell you anything about the plant's description.

Sometimes after the genus we see "spp." This simply means "species" and indicates that the species is either not known or is unimportant, or that the description refers to all the species of that genera. For example, "*Pinus* spp." refers to all pines, or either the species is unknown.

See how many plants you can name in your neighborhood or at a local nursery. Learn to know them by sight and try to spot them as you ride down the road. Don't try this during knock-off traffic, though, you might get knocked off yourself. Call the name out loud each time you recognize one. Good luck, and remember that knowing plants by their names is the first step in enjoying the outdoors and the exciting world of horticulture.

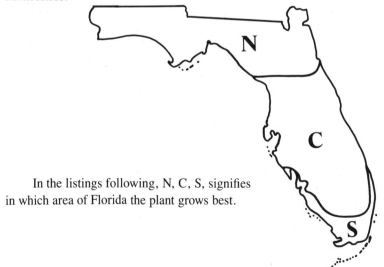

In the listings following, N, C, S, signifies in which area of Florida the plant grows best.

TEN POPULAR GROUND COVERS

These plants never grow more than a foot in height and look best when planted in masses around an accent plant or bordering a flower bed.

1. Ajuga *(A. reptans)* N, C: Ajuga, or bugleweed, seldom grows over three inches tall, but creeps slowly across the ground and makes a dense mat for bordering a bed or planting amongst stepping stones. It withstands light foot traffic. Has a purple-bronze color. I really like this one.

2. Sprengeri Fern *(Asparagus sprengeri)* N, C; One of the fastest growing of the bushy covers, up to one foot tall. Planted two feet apart, it makes a thick, feathery cover in one year. My favorite for low maintenance.

3. Fig Marigold *(Glottiphyllum depressum)* C, S: A succulent runner for cactus garden appearance. Covers bed in one season. I like to use it in rock gardens. Likes sun and sand. Grows to six inches.

4. Juniper *(Juniperus* spp.) N, C: Two popular junipers for ground covers are shore juniper, a salt-tolerant species up to one foot tall, and bar harbor juniper, a three-inch-tall variety for a slow, but dense, evergreen cover. These are cold-hardy but should be sprayed periodically with a mixture of Kelthane and copper for mites and fungus. Also look for the three-inch-high horizontal juniper and the thick-trunked San Jose variety.

5. Oyster Plant *(Rhoeo discolor)* C, S: A colorful spear-like plant with showy purple leaves, often used at the base of taller specimen plants with similar textured leaves such as palms, yucca, dracena, or screw pine. Sun or shade is okay. Interesting color plant.

6. Wandering Jew *(Zebrina pendula)* C, S: A good color cover with leaves purple underneath and striped green and white on top. Does best in shade and rich soil. Will freeze at temperatures below 28°F. A succulent herb that creeps vigorously in summer and makes a cover up to four inches. A similar creeper, purple queen, has smaller leaves that are entirely purple.

OYSTER PLANT

WANDERING JEW

WEDELIA

Shore Juniper—*Juniperus conferta*

Ivy—*Hedera* **spp.**

7. Wedelia *(W. trilobata)* C, S: A fast, vigorous creeper that grows to 18 inches. Often grown on ditch banks or around base of trees where lawn mower cannot reach. Has light green, tender leaves and occasionally small, yellow flowers. Give it plenty of room to spread.

8. Ivy *(Hedera* spp.) N, C, S: Numerous varieties exist with assorted leaf shapes. English ivy and Algerian ivy are the two most popular species. Ivies are hardy, deep green, and grow in sun or shade. Will climb on a wall or creep on the ground. A yearly mowing in the early spring is often beneficial.

9. Liriope *(L. muscari)* N, C, S: An ornamental grass with wide blades and spikes of blue flowers in the spring. Grows to one foot in clumps or, after several years, forms a solid bed. Makes a good border plant for walks and drives. Prefers some shade. Plant the variegated (green and white) variety for interesting color contrast.

10. Dicondra *(D. carolinensis)* N, C, S: A creeping, round-leaf, dense cover seldom over one inch tall. An excellent grass substitute. Withstands heavy foot traffic. Grows anywhere, but may get a fungus that is hard to control. Never needs mowing.

Also look for these good ground covers: lantana, assorted ferns, artillery plant, peperomia, mondo grass, alternanthera. Your local nurseryman can show you most of them and describe their growing habits.

TEN HEDGE PLANTS

Hedge plants listed here are those which form the most dense visual barrier, but do not produce conspicuous flowers, they look best in mass or rows and are rarely planted alone. Many flowering shrubs make good hedge barriers, but they are reserved for the list of flowering shrubs. These hedge plants hold their leaves year-round and will grow to just about any height or width to which you train them.

1. Viburnum *(V. odoratissimum & V. suspensum)* N, C, S: Fast-growing, withstand cold, drought, and shade. Two of my favorites.

2. Ligustrum *(L. lucidum)* N, C, S: Glossy, deep green leaves withstand any condition except wet feet. Plant high and watch it grow. Several yellow-leaf varieties also available.

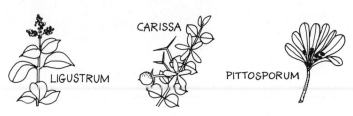

LIGUSTRUM   CARISSA   PITTOSPORUM

Viburnum—*V. suspensum*

3. Carissa *(C. grandiflora)* C, S: Likes full sun. Slower growing but interesting shape for character. Plant Boxwood Beauty for a two- to three-foot variety. Red golf-ball size fruit makes a tropical jelly. Call your local Extension Home Economist for recipes.

4. Podocarpus *(P.* spp.*)* N, C, S: One of the best small-leaf hedges for a fine-textured appearance. Too often planted at corners of homes. Doesn't like wet feet. Stands shade or sun.

5. Pittosporum *(P. tobira)* N, C, S: Nice texture and interesting odor from crushed leaves. Does best on north side of house where there is shade. Comes in green or green-and-white variegated. I plant it where low maintenance is required.

6. Coral Ardisia *(A. crenata)* N, C: Produces attractive clusters of red berries (sometimes white). A handsome shrub that should be planted in the shade.

7. Holly *(Ilex* spp.*)* N, C, S: Numerous hollies grow throughout Florida. *Rotunda* has prickly leaves, *burfordi* does not, yaupon has very small leaves, gallberry is taller-growing and is more native. All tolerate sun or shade.

8. Australian Pine*(Casuarina equisetifolia)* C, S: A dense, feathery hedge plant that makes an open fifty-foot barrier where tall borders are desired. Often seen on beach property. Frequent pruning will keep it down to six feet.

9. Juniper *(Juniperus* spp.*)* N, C: For a tall variety, choose *hetzi.* Pfitzer juniper is one of the best sprawlers. Blue Vase is compact and makes a good showing when planted behind springeri fern. Spray occassionally for mites and leaf spot disease.

10. Severinia *(S. buxifolia)* N, C, S: For a truly impenetrable barrier, plant this thorny, small-leafed variety every thirty inches along a border. It does not usually grow more than five or six feet tall.

Other hedge plants to look for include arborvitae, aralia, jasmine, eugenia, malpighia, orange jasmine.

TEN SHRUBS FOR COLOR

These plants are more showy when planted in masses of six or more to create a real eye-stopper, but show restraint, the eye needs to rest sometime. They can, of course, be used as hedge plants. Plant gallon-size plants three feet apart. Heights vary up to ten feet.

1. Ixora *(I. coccinea)* C, S: Produces brilliant red flowers throughout most of the warmer months when pruned only in the fall. Very popular plant.

2. Azalea *(Rhododendron* spp.*)* N, C: Flowers of white, pink or red. For 18-inch plants with long blooming season, choose Duc de Rohan. Others bloom only in spring. Available also in dwarfs (under one foot) or up to eight feet tall.

IXORA   AZALEA   OLEANDER   PLUMBAGO

3. Oleander *(Nerium oleander)* N, C, S: Very large shrub with sparse foliage and either red, white, or pink flowers. Does well in sunny locations and poor soil. Spray Sevin for caterpillars. Don't burn this poisonous plant. Harmless to touch.

4. Plumbago *(P. capensis)* C, S: Blue-white inflorescences appear during warmer months of the year. Sprawling habit of growth. I'm fond of this one where a two- to three-foot hedge is needed.

5. Croton *(Codiaeum variegatum)* C, S: No flowers but large, richly variegated leaves of red, purple orange, green, white, and yellow make this the most colorful shrub in the world. Buy only the colorful varieties.

6. Copperleaf *(Acalypha wilkesiana)* C, S: Brilliant, large, red-bronze leaves make this plant a popular color choice. Leaves drop if winters reach temperatures in the low 30s.

7. Sinensis *(Ligustrum sinesis)* N, C, S: Small, white leaves on this variegated privet make it an excellent contrast to set off red or green plants growing alongside.

8. Yellow Ligustrum *(L. howardi)* N, C, S: This and newer variegated varieties produce yellow leaves that are noticed from great distances.

CROTON   TIBOUCHINA   HIBUSCUS

9. Tibouchina *(T. semidecandia)* N, C, S: Large-growing broadleaf evergreen producing colorful purple flowers in the summer. Popular and makes quite a showing.

10. Hibiscus *(H. rosa-sinensis)* N, C, S: Large colorful flowers of several hundred varieties popularly picked for indoor use. Singles and doubles available in red, pink, white, yellow, apricot.

Also look for these colorful plants: bottlebrush, powderpuff, camellia, gardenia, golden dewdrop, hydrangea, Turk's cap, angel's trumpet, cassia, poinsettia, yellow shrimp plant, and thryallis.

TEN COLORFUL FLOWERS

Flowers look good planted in pockets of larger beds. The majority of the flowers listed below grow as annuals throughout the state, that is, they are planted as seed in the spring or fall, bloom a long season and then die, all in a twelve-month period. Some, however, such as the periwinkle, may live and flower year-round depending on the degree of cold. Those that do not die are called perennials. (Note: No scientific names are listed for flowers as they are not generally used in the trade.)

1. Periwinkle: A two-foot perennial wildflower that blooms almost year-round where other plants starve out. No maintenance is required. Dies back in cold portions of the state.

Periwinkle

2. Stoke's Aster: One of Florida's best perennials. Clumps produce blue flowers on one-foot high stalks in the summer. Pink, yellow, and white varieties are available.

3. Strawflower: These robust annuals are seeded in early spring and grow to three freet. I like to dry them for indoor use. Cut stem when bud is half open, strip off leaves, and hang upside down in a shady, well-ventilated place. A variety of colors are available.

4. Rose Moss: Also called portulaca, this brilliant summer annual is unequaled as a rock garden plant. Flowers of brilliant, gay colors open in the morning and close in the afternoon. Thrives under trying conditions of drought, heat, and poor soil.

5. Dianthus: A variety of frilly flower shapes and colors are available with dianthus (pinks). This fall annual will produce a second bloom if they are cut back and fertilized.

6. Petunia: Undoubtedly the most popular winter annual in Florida due to the numerous colors available today. Profuse blooms from fall-planted plants adorn the landscape until hot weather burns them out.

7. Pansies: Numerous colorful varieties make this delicate beauty a favorite also. Plant where a low, colorful border is desired. Blooms in winter and spring months when seeded in fall.

8. Marigolds: With petunias the number one winter annual, mari-

Rose Moss

golds take the spotlight for summer blooms. Varieties are yellow, orange, and red, from six inches to three feet tall. A profuse bloomer.

9. Canna: An excellent backdrop where a tall border is needed. Spikes of pink, yellow, and red may be cut in the spring for cut flowers. Little attention is required other than keeping competitive weeds controlled.

10. Tulip Poppy: Also called *hunnemania,* it is much like the California poppy. They grow and spread easily but transplant with difficulty. Plants are two feet and produce yellow flowers for cutting.

For other colorful flowers try: calendula, alyssum, begonia, chrysanthemum, nasturtium, sunflower, impatiens, Shasta daisy.

SEVEN NATIVE SHADE TREES

Shade trees planted on the home site are the most permanent of all landscape plants. Therefore much thought and investigation is in order before selecting varieties. For years I have suggested that the native trees are the best choice because they are better equipped to resist adverse elements in the environment. They have a will to survive on their own that keeps maintenance down. Locate shade trees to provide afternoon shade on the house or patio. These trees grow throughout most of the state.

1. Oaks (*Quercus* spp.): The laurel oak is perhaps the most popular.

A steady grower, strong, good shape. Sheds leaves briefly in spring. The live oak is the most picturesque with undulating limbs and tough, cupped leaves. Both grow to about fifty feet.

2. Elm (*Ulmus* spp.) Many species grow to varying heights and make excellent shade trees. Elms have a lacy appearance because of the small size of their leaves. Leaves have toothed margins and a lopsided base.

3. Southern Magnolia (*Magnolia grandiflora*): A large sturdy grower with huge white blossoms; flowers sparsely in summer. Tree shape is usually pyramidal with limbs growing to the ground. Leaves stay on tree year-round.

4. Tulip Tree (*Liriodendron tulipifera*): Corky projections on the stems help identify this nicely shaped tree. Leaves fall in winter. Does not do well in South Florida.

5. Sycamore (*Platanus occidentalis*): Also called buttonwood, perhaps the largest of all deciduous trees in Florida. Grows fast in Central and North Florida. Splotched trunk for added interest.

6. Maple (*Acer floridanum*): The Florida maple much resembles the popular sugar maple of the North, but leaves do not become so colorful in the fall. Trunk turns grey with age. We enjoy raking leaves with the kids.

7. Gumbolimbo (*Bursera simaruba*): One of the largest and most common trees of South Florida. Leaves drop in fall. Grows up to fifty feet, with a trunk two to three feet in diameter.

Other trees grown in Florida for shade include: silk oak, Cuban laurel, eucalyptus, golden rain (yellow flowers), chinaberry, weeping fig, camphor, jacaranda (purple flowers), and carrotwood.

King Sago—*Cycas revoluta* (female in foreground; male in background)

TEN ACCENT PLANTS

Accent plants are specimen plants usually three to ten feet tall, but can be much larger. They are often planted along in the middle of a massed ground cover or shrub bed where they receive no aesthetic competition.

Often unique in character, accent plants should be the main focal point in a particular part of the yard.

1. King Sago *(Cycas revoluta)* N, C: Used where a short, stiff, somewhat formal appearance is desired. Quite attractive.

2. Italian Cypress *(Cupressus sempervirens)* N, C: Best in clumps of three or in a row spaced several feet apart for a formal effect. Arrow straight, it is only two feet wide and up to thirty feet tall. Cut out top at any desired height.

3. Pampus Grass *(Cortaderis selloana)* N, C, S: Beautiful clump of five-foot grass with showy, silver plumes in warmer months.

4. Schefflera *(Brassaia actinophylla)* C, S: Small, narrow tree with large, finger-like leaves. Cut out top at desired height. Nice for a Spanish effect.

Dracena–*Dracaena* spp.

Torulosa Juniper–*Juniperus torulosa*

5. Dracena (*Dracaena* spp.) C, S: Numerous species available. Usually thumb-size trunks terminating in miniature, palm-like clusters of lance-shaped leaves. *Marginata* and red dracena are popular.

6. Screw Pine (*Pandanus utilis*) C, S: After growing a few feet tall, they send numerous aerial roots to the ground that look like legs. I find them very attractive.

7. Norfolk Island Pine (*Araucaria excelsa*) C, S: From four to forty feet. A stately specimen pine with spoke-like branches. If lower branches die out, plant pfitzer juniper around the trunk. Everyone likes this one.

8. Pigmy Date Palm (*Phoenix` roebelenii*) C, S: Also called Roebeleni palm. A much used, but still attractive palm. Plant singly or in groups of two or three. Height about five feet.

9. Areca Palm (*Chrysalidocarpus lutescens*) C, S: Tender for North Florida but used where greater heights are required. A clump palm with numerous wrist-size, bamboo-shaped trunks that appear yellowish in the sun. Grows best in shade.

10. Torulosa Juniper *(Juniperus torulosa)* N, C: Unique upright shape reminds me of Van Gogh's cypress trees. Good character. Up to eight feet.

TEN EXOTICS FOR PATIO TUBS

Exotic plants are tropical in appearance, and while they are listed here as tub plants, many do just as well planted in the ground. Plants in patio tubs should be treated as accent plants and can be used to frame a patio. Be sure to check on their tolerance to cold in your area. In tubs they can be brought into the protection of a garage on those extra cold nights.

1. Elephant's Ear *(Xanthosoma* spp.): Gigantic leaves spill forth on three to four foot stems. Often seen on ditch banks growing in the wild. I sometimes plant them at the back border to tower over short plants.

ELEPHANT'S EAR   DIEFFENBACHIA   PONY TAIL

2. Dieffenbachia *(Dieffenbachia* spp.): Also called dumb cane because of the poisonous sap in the leaves. Keep away from small children. A very attractive, large-leafed, variegated tropical with succulent growth.

3. Bamboo Palm *(Chamaedorea* spp.): A leafy palm called Chamaedorea. Does best in shade. Protect from cold. We use them in darker portions of the house.

4. Pony Tail *(Beaucarnea recurvata)* Four to six-foot plants have a basketball-shaped trunk sitting in the soil surface. Protruding from this is a narrow stem that terminates in a splash of long, grasslike leaves of lacy character. I really like it.

5. Bird of Paradise *(Strelitzia reginae):* A popular, sword-like plant grown in three-foot clusters. Potash helps to bring out the colorful orange and blue flowers that resemble a bird in flight.

6. Shefflera *(S. actinophylla):* A leafy tub plant sometimes called umbrella tree and grown as an accent plant. Will stand sun or shade and can be kept small by cutting the top out. A good poolside plant.

7. Weeping Fig *(Ficus benjamina):* In landscape it makes an appealing shade tree. One of the most popular plants used in living room photos seen in various home and garden magazines. Store-bought plants should be acclimated to semi-shade for sixty days before bringing into darker shade indoors to prevent them from dropping their leaves.

8. Fiddleleaf Fig *(Ficus lyrata):* Another of the large fig family that does well as a tub plant. Large, somewhat fiddleshaped leaves are very attractive. May be grown as a shade tree in protected areas (will not take freeze).

9. Yucca *(Y. aloifolia):* A dangerously sharp-pointed; upright grower that is eye-appealing in masses. Spineless varieties are available for use around the patio. A common practice is to place cut styrofoam egg cartons on the sharp points to simulate flowers. This practice produces a tacky, artificial appearance in the landscape.

10. Century Plant *(Agave americana):* Similar to yucca but much broader and without trunk. These and other Agave species produce a very tall flower spike that drains the mother plant to death. However, young plants continue to come up from the root system.

There are numerous other exotics that can be used in tubs or in the landscape to produce a tropical affect. Ask your nurseryman to show you: splitleaf philodendron, rubber plant, monstera, rice paper plant, aloe, billbergia, ginger fern, lady palm, and papyrus.

TEN CLIMBING VINES

As a general rule of thumb, the vines which drop their leaves in cold weather are the ones which grow the fastest and need much room. The slower growers are often evergreen. Many vines are used as ground cover if the area is not to be walked on. Learn to recognize these popular vines. You can see them at your local nursery or botanical garden.

1. Syngonium *(S. podophyllum)* C, S: You can buy this little plant in stores that have the rack of houseplants in two-to three-inch pots. The spear-shaped leaves grow to two feet across as it towers up a tree trunk outdoors. Available in green or variegated.

2. Pothos (*Scindapsus* spp.) S: Many call this plant "hunter's robe" or "variegated philodendron" because it looks like the little heart-shaped philodendron popularly grown indoors, but that is incorrect. Plant at the base of a tall pine tree and watch the leaves get enormous and beautifully variegated. Needs shade.

3. Creeping Fig *(Ficus pumila)* N, C, S: Clings to any surface and is often seen on brick walls and buildings as the southern "halls of ivy." Evergreen ivy with small leaves. Sun or shade.

4. Allamanda *(A. cathartica)* C, S: Poisonous to eat, but who eats them? Very popular for its showy yellow trumpet-shaped flowers during the long warm season. Needs to be tied.

5. Bougainvillea (*B.* spp.) C, S: Brilliant red flowers smother this rampant grower. Bougainvillea as well as allamanda will make a shrub if cut back. Give it lots of room, preferably at the back border. An extra dose of bloom fertilizer (2-10-10 analysis) will prolong the blooming season.

6. Bower Vine *(Pandorea ricasoliana)* C, S: Also called *pandorea.* White flowers not too showy. Lush green leaves take a light freeze. Twines, does not cling.

7. Philodendron (*P.* spp.) C, S: Numerous species are available for protected locations in the shade. We have *P. floridum* and *P. rubrum* growing up our pine trees and enjoy them both.

8. Mexican Flame Vine *(Senecio confusus)* C, S: A sprawling vine needing support that grows most anywhere. Produces one-inch orange flowers in great abundance during warmer months.

BOUGAINVILLEA

MEXICAN FLAME VINE

CONFEDERATE JASMINE

9. Confederate Jasmine *(Trachelospermum jasminides)* N, C, S: Popular for the abundant small, star-shaped flowers from April on. Too often grown on light poles in front lawn.

10. Mandevilla *(Dipladenia splendens)* C, S: Also sold under the name *Dipladenia* or pink allamanda. Similar to allamanda flowers, only these are pink trumpets. The vine twines up a string trellis for a beautiful showing.

EIGHT SMALL TREES

Small trees are useful in Florida for the small property and as accent plants on larger property. In the latter case they should be planted close to the house with larger trees reserved for the border. Here are several excellent choices that grow from fifteen to thirty feet in height. Many fruit trees may also be used in the small location.

1. Wax Myrtle *(Myrica cerifera)* N, C, S: One of my favorite choices for year-round green foliage and low maintenance. No flowers.

2. American Holly *(Ilex opaca)* N, C: Attractive red berries in the winter make this a favorite of cooler climates. Many varieties available with or without prickly leaves. Dahoon holly is an N, C, S species with smaller leaves and an affinity for wet locations;

3. India Rosewood *(Dalbergia sissoo)* C, S: I enjoy watching the lacy leaves dance with the slightest breeze. No flowers, though. Another very similar plant is the Chinese tallow tree. Either is a good choice where an oriental effect is desired.

4. Dogwood *(Cornus florida)* N, C: Rarely seen south of Tampa Bay. The attractive white or red flowers appear on bare branches in the late winter of North Florida. An old-time favorite.

5. Royal Poinciana *(Delonix regia)* C, S: Rarely seen north of Tampa Bay. Brilliant red flowers flood the top of this umbrella-shaped tree to inspire the famous song "Poinciana." The pride of the tropics loses its leaves in winter adding further variety to the landscape.

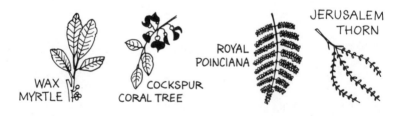

6. Cockspur Coral Tree *(Erythrina cristagallii)* C, S: A semi-evergreen (drops its leaves only if temperature gets near freezing) that produces brilliant crimson flowers for the winter landscape.

7. Jerusalem Thorn *(Parkinsonia aculeata)* N, C, S: This deciduous tree has small, delightfully yellow flowers beginning in spring and continuing throughout the summer. The leaves are lacy and stringy, much like a weeping willow. Watch out for the thorns, though.

8. Dwarf Elm *(Ulmus pumila)* N, C: Fast grower with good spread.

Leaves are lacey, semi-evergreen, but have no flowers. Weeping species are available that I find very attractive.

Also look for acacia, punk, bischofia chaste, cherry laurel, frangipani, loquat, redbud, shaving brush, and tabebuia.

PALMS FOR THE FLORIDA LANDSCAPE

Florida has a marvelous selection of palm trees. Some have palmate fronds like fan palms; others have long pinnate leaves that dance in the slightest breeze. some grow in clumps; others as a single trunk specimen. Most all produce bee-attracting flowers and fruit from date size to coconut. Listed are several of the more popular ones.

NAME	HEIGHT	FRONDS	TRUNK	MISCELLANEOUS
1. Coconut Palm (Cocos nucifera)	80 ft.	12 ft. pinnate	single	curved trunk, very majestic
2. Everglades Palm (Paurotis wrightii)	30 ft.	fan	clump	good for home property
3. Cabbage Palm (Pseudophoenix sargentii)	40 ft.	fan	single	old fronds create lattice trunk
4. Cocos Plumosa (Arecastrum roman-zoffianum)	40 ft.	pinnate	single	most common for landscape
5. Cocos Australis (Butia capitata)	25 ft.	pinnate	fat single	curved, C-shaped fronds sweeping to ground
6. Canary Island Date Palm (Phoenix canariensis)	20-50 ft.	pinnate with 30 ft. spread	fat single	trunk looks like a huge pineapple
7. Phoenix reclinata	50 ft.	pinnate and thorny	clump	most attractive when older
8. Pigmy Date Palm (Phoenix roebelinii)	2-6 ft.	small pinnate	single	graceful for door-yard
9. Royal Palm (Roystonea elata)	60 ft.	pinnate	single	smooth white trunk, very attractive
10. Chinese Fan Palm (Livistona chinensis)	25 ft.	fan	single	tips of fronds weep
11. European Fan Palm (Chamaerops humilis)	6 ft.	fan	single	quite hardy
12. Washington Palm (Washingtonia robusta)	60 ft.	fan	single	for avenue planting or around two-story buildings
13. Queen Sago Palm (Cycas circiniles)	25 ft.	pinnate	single	dark green lacy fronds
14. King Sago Palm (Cycas revoluta)	3-6 ft.	pinnate	single	short, stiff fronds hardy
15. Areca (Chrysalidocarpus lutescens)	25 ft.	pinnate	clump	bamboo-like trunks plant in shade

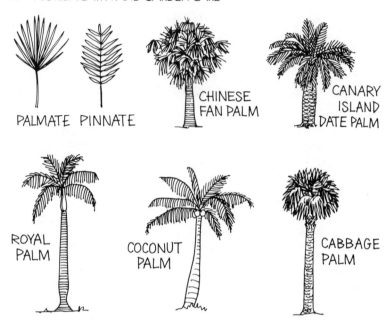

SALT TOLERANT PLANTS

The degree of salt tolerance in plants has puzzled many home gardeners. The literature on the subject is often in disagreement, and there are many exceptions to the rule. Several reasons exist for this uncertainty: each plant, although of the same species, is a unique individual with different degrees of tolerance. Often it is not actually the salt that causes the damage but rather the driving winds carrying fine particles of sand to cut and blast, or actually tear limbs from the plant; the constant warm winds associated with beach conditions tend to dry out plants; soil conditions are often so sandy that the roots require watering twice a day; at other times, the soil is filled with shells that keeps the pH very alkaline causing the plants to starve to death; and in certain cases the plants may be protected from these conditions in varying degrees that are not readily obvious to the brown thumb gardener.

Before choosing plants for a seaside home, consult the list of plants generally used in beach conditions. The plants marked with a (D) tolerate the dune conditions where strong wind, blasting sand, and salt spray are common. The others may be planted in more protected locations around

Salt Tolerant Plants

GROUND COVERS

alternanthera
aspargus fern
Euonymous fortunei (D)
Ficus radicans (D)
fig marigold (D)
Algerian ivy (D)
English ivy
shore juniper
Kalanchoe spp.
weeping lantana (D)
Liriope spp.
mondo
portulaca
Virginia creeper (D)
Sanseveria spp. (D)
Sedum spp. (D)
purple queen
cape honeysuckle
oyster plant
caltrops (D)
wedelia (D)
wandering Jew
cuphea
dwarf yaupon holly (D)

PALMS

Acrocomia
Cocos australis (Butia)
European fan
coconut (D)
silver palm
hurricane palm
African oil palm
gingerbread
Lantania
Chinese fan
bottle palm
Paurotis wrightii
Canary Island Date
date
Phoenix reclinata
fan palm
royal palm
cabbage palm (D)
windmill palm
Christmas palm
Washingtonia robusta (D)

SHRUBS

acacia (D)
adhatoda (D)
copper leaf
century plant (D)
salt bush (D)
boxwood
bottlebrush (D)
carissa (D)
night-blooming jasmine
coco plum (D)
sea grape (D)
dracena (D)
thorny elaeagnus (D)
crown of thorns
pencil tree (D)
Fatsia japonica
pineapple guava
Gardenia jasminoides
hibiscus
yaupon holly (D)
ixora
crape myrtle
common lantana (D)
Texas sage
ligustrum (D)
holly malpighia
Turk's cap
wax myrtle (D)
oleander (D)
devil's backbone
pittosporum (D)
plumbago
podocarpus
pyracantha (D)
rhapiolepsis
box thorn
arborvitae
Viburnam suspensum
Yucca spp.
coontie
eugenia
red cedar (D)

TREES

Norfolk Island pine (D)
black olive (D)
gumbolimbo
weeping bottlebrush
Australian pine (D)
pitch apple (D)
pigeon plum (D)
buttonwood (D)
geiger tree (D)
Dalbergia sissoo
royal poinciana
eucalyptus (D)
Ficus spp.
sea hibiscus (D)
golden rain
magnolia
punks (D)
wax myrtle (D)
ochrosia
Jerusalem thorn (D)
mangrove
pine (D)
pongamia
laurel oak
water oak
live oak
Brazilian pepper
mahogany
seaside mahoe
carrotwood

VINES

allamanda
bougainvillea
trumpet vine (D)
Cassia bicapsularis
winter creeper (D)
creeping fig (D)
night blooming cereus (D)
hedge cactus
morning glory (D)
downy jasmine
Japanese honeysuckle
flame vine (D)
Pothos (hunter's robe)
palmetto (D)
brittle thatch (D)

the beach property. Beach dweller's whose homes are several blocks from the ocean should remember that on misty nights salt may be carried several blocks from the dunes and deposited on foliage. To protect them, even from these conditions, many plants are adapted with hairy leaves; others have a thick cutin layer creating high gloss on leaves or stems. Still others have leaves formed as crusty fish-like scales. Washing the tops of seaside plants after a misty night will increase the health of most plants. Check with your nurseryman for availability in your area.

The identification of Florida landscape plants is a field of study in itself. But without going too deeply I have here listed the most popular ones seen around Florida homes. For a further study, may I suggest you secure a copy of *Florida Landscape Plants* by John V. Watkins (Gainesville: University of Florida Press) or *500 Plants of South Florida* by Julia F. Morton (Miami: Fairchild Tropical Garden) both of which are available at your favorite bookstore or directly from the publishers.

This concludes the plant identification chapter. Be sure to visit a nursery and ask to see these plants to help you learn to call them by name. In chapter six we will see how these plants can be used in the landscape to beautify your home.

CHAPTER FIVE

How to Grow
Your Own Plants

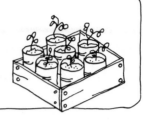

To me, the most exciting area of home gardening is growing my own plants. Did you ever snitch a leaf or twig from a choice plant, smuggle it home, and try to grow it? (Sure you have – I've seen you.) I have a hint for you. Roll the cutting in a damp paper towel and place it inside a plastic bag. In this manner you can carry it around in your pocket a couple of days. But, did you snitch the right part and what are you going to do with it when you get home? That is the interesting question.

Seeding is one method of growing your own plants. It is, of course, a sexual method (asexual methods will be explained later) of reproduction, and therefore, the offspring might be slightly different from the parent. We see this offspring variation in children and their parents. To duplicate the parent plant exactly, asexual propagation must be used. But first let's explore the world of:

GROWING PLANTS FROM SEED

Beneath its protective coat, a seed contains an embryo and nourishing tissue which feeds the growing embryo until it sends forth roots and leaves to make its own food. When planted, moisture and heat (light is not required) dissolve the hard coat in a few days, allowing the embryo to penetrate the shell and grow. To store seeds, simply reverse the elements by keeping the surrounding environment dry and cool. Dust with captan and Sevin to eliminate fungus and insects during the storage period.

On some seeds, the protective coating being so hard, scarification is required. This is achieved by filing the hard seed coat or soaking it in boiling water.

Seeds come from fruit, the base of the flower.

How to Plant Seeds

You can germinate seeds most any place: on a window sill, in the ground, wherever there is moisture and warmth.

Seeds should be planted in rows to facilitate handling. Be sure to use a sterile soil mix. To sterilize your own soil, place a damp, two-inch layer on a cookie sheet and heat in a 200-degree oven for 45 minutes. However, the simplest method is to use clean builders sand (not salty sand from the beach) or vermiculite bought from a garden supply store. Place the mix in a nursery flat, sow seeds, then water with a fine mist until mix is moist throughout.

In a few weeks, after all seeds are germinated, carefully lift the tender seedlings and transplant them to small, two-to four-inch pots.

Place the potted plants in partial sunlight (the filtered shade of a tree is a good location) for one month. Fertilize weekly with a complete, liquid fertilizer available from garden supply stores. The soil mix in the pot should not be pure vermiculite. Use sterile potting soil available in small bags.

After one month, harden off plants by placing in full sun and grow until the roots begin to crowd the pot. By this time, plants are hardy and healthy and can either be transplanted to a more permanent pot or placed directly in the ground.

How Deep to Plant

In warm Florida soils, planting depth is not too critical. But seeds do have their preference:

1. Large seeds, the size of a pea, should be planted at a depth three to four times their thickness.

2. Small seeds, the size of a pin head, should be planted at a depth twice their thickness.

3. Very tiny seeds often do best if not buried but scattered on the surface and gently watered.

GROWING PLANTS VEGETATIVELY

Vegetative propagation is a method by which some portion of the parent plant is cut and made to grow into a new plant. Vegetative propagation is an asexual method of reproduction. It requires no flowers and no pollination. There are four good reasons why plants are grown vegetatively instead of by seed:

1. *To duplicate for standardization* – Nurserymen who want to produce thousands of plants exactly alike for landscape use choose vegetative methods. Most plants grown from seed lose their desired characteristics due to Mendel's law of degeneration.

2. *Only way sometimes* – Often with such plants as gardenia, Florida cherry, and St. Augustine grass, viable seed is not produced sufficiently so new plants *must* be grown vegetatively.

3. Germination may be difficult – With such plants as holly and rose, germination of seed is too difficult.

4. More economical – Vegetative propagation is usually much faster and tends to keep retail prices competitively low.

How to Build a Miniature Rooting Bed

A small unit for rooting just a few plants can be made as pictured.

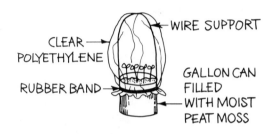

A sealed unit such as this will never need watering. Once it is set up, forget it for a month or two. When plants start to show new growth, remove cover, add a little liquid fertilizer and move to a brighter location. Leave plant in the gallon can to grow for one full season before setting out in the landscape. I find it useful to throw a handful or milorganite or cow manure into the top two inches of each gallon can during the "growing on" period.

Don't fertilize a cutting
before it has grown roots.

Five Ways to Propagate

Each of these five methods of propagating has its own advantages. Remember, they are all vegetative, or asexual, methods as opposed to seeding.

1. Rooting cutting: Always use a sharp knife or hand pruner to cut stems from plants. Make a clean cut on a stem four to six inches long. The best cuttings are taken from the ends of *new* growth when the lower half of the cutting has become woody. However, on many shrubs and trees several cuttings along a stem may be made. Just be sure to plant them base end down. Otherwise, the law of polarity will not allow them to root. Before rooting woody plants, I find it helpful to wound the

cutting by scraping the bark from two narrow strips, one inch from the base. Dip this exposed wood in a powdered rooting hormone available from garden supply stores. Be sure to shake all excess powder from the cutting before placing it upright on a flat of vermiculite. Space one inch apart.

If cuttings are to be made from house plants or vines that do not have woody stems, the process is the same except the wounding and hormone treatment are omitted. These succulent plants often root very rapidly. Many house plants can be rooted in water. Most will also root from leaf cuttings. A stem cutting with several leaves, however, will make a larger plant once it is rooted.

In sunny Florida, cuttings are made any time of the year. However, rooting is faster during the summer months when growth is rapid and the soil is warm.

2. Layering: The most popular method is called *air layering.* A healthy, vigorous, finger-size limb is chosen and wounded (remove a strip of bark one inch long and three-quarters way around the limb). Wrap this wound with a handful of damp sphagnum moss. Secure the moss with clear plastic or tin foil and tie it snuggly above and below

wrapped area. After several weeks remove the foil and the sphagnum will be filled with new roots. Cut the rooted stem below the roots and plant in a pot or in the ground. These roots should never be allowed to dry out, so keep the foil tightly wrapped and check it periodically for moisture retention. I have found that applying a rooting hormone to the wound speeds rooting of most layering. Air layering is also called *marcottage* and *mossing off.*

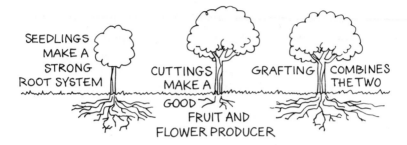

3. *Grafting:* When some flowering and fruiting plants are grown from seed, the new plant reverts back to a wilder variety. These wild forms often have sour fruit and small flowers of poor fragrance. Yet, when the flowering or fruiting plant is grown from a cutting it possesses the desirable features but has a weak root system, susceptible to nematodes and root diseases. The best solution is to remove the above-ground portion of the rooted cutting and graft it to the root system of the disease-resistant, wild seedling.

To graft a mango, plant a seed one inch deep and concave side down. When the plant has grown one-foot you will have the makings of a vigorous root system, but the tree will produce only shade and not much fruit.

The next step is to cut a stem tip of the same diameter as your one-foot-tall plant from a neighbor's tree. Be sure to choose a tree that produces delicious fruit and is just beginning to flush out new, reddish leaves. Wedge the two plants together as shown in the illustration. Be

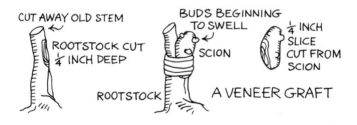

very careful that the moist layer just under the bark matches on both the rootstock and on your neighbor's cutting (scion). It is sort of like matching veins with a finger transplant. Secure the graft with a tight band, and soon the top will grow and develop into an excellent tree, just like your neighbor's, while the rootstock will develop into a vigorous, disease-resistant root system – perfect combination. When growth begins, cut away the stem of the rootstock plant just above the graft.

4. *Budding:* This technique is similar to grafting. Begin with a seedling (a plant grown from seed) just as if you were grafting. When the trunk becomes ½ inch in diameter, it is ready to be budded. Budding is best done in early spring, late spring, or late summer when the sap is flowing and the bark is loose.

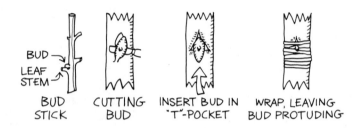

BUD
LEAF
STEM

BUD STICK   CUTTING BUD   INSERT BUD IN "T"-POCKET   WRAP, LEAVING BUD PROTUDING

Cut a bud stick from a neighbor's tree. Be sure to choose a limb of relatively new growth. A bud stick is simply a pruned twig supporting several leaves. There is a bud tucked in the crotch just above each leaf.

Now, cut an inverted "T" into the bark of your rootstock plant about four inches above the ground. From your bud stick, first cut off a leaf leaving ¼ inch of its stem intact, then cut the entire bud away as shown. This bud chip should be about 1½ inches long. Next, simply slip the bud chip up into the "T"-pocket, wrap securely with a rubber band, and prune the top out of the rootstock plant to force the bud to grow.

Many people like to bud several different varieties such as oranges, grapefruits, and tangerines all on one rootstock. This works as long as you take the scion from plants of the same genus as the rootstock.

5. *Separation or Division:* Plants propagated by separation are those in which the mother plant produces a growth structure that can be easily removed and grown on as an individual plant. these growth structures

DIVISION OF BANANA   SHOOTS FROM SAGO PALM   CUT AND REMOVE RUNNERS OF FERN

BREAK AWAY

may be bulbs (amaryllis), corms (gladiolus), tubers (caladiums), rhizomes (canna, bamboo), offsets (pineapple, king sago palm, cactus), runners (strawberry, fern, ajuga), or suckers (banana, agave). Your job is simply to dig and divide as with banana or to break off the offsets and re-root them. Division is the simplest form of propagation and is a rewarding technique to the novice. Separating runners is familiar to most plant enthusiasts.

Every home gardener should try some method of propagation because of the great lesson on plant needs that is to be learned. Those pale-green thumbers who never dirty their fingers, never absorb the knowledge that comes from growing a plant from its bud or seed stage to its reproductive stage. It is like understanding people better after you have raised a house full of them from birth.

Following, is a list of plants and how they can be propagated. Experiment in as many methods of propagation as you desire.

PLANTS PROPAGATED BY:

Seed	Stem Cuttings	Leaf Cuttings	Trench Layering
Annual flowers, vegetables, palms	Most any woody tree or shrub. Most house plants.	begonia African violet pepperomia sanseveria	weeping willow Most any vine viburnam
Mound Layering	**Air Layering**	**Grafting**	**Budding**
croton tibouchina powderpuff	rubber plant oleander camellia screw pine dracena	mango avocado gardenia carambola	citrus trees rose pear peach
Separation	**Division**		
sago palms caladium amaryllis cactus pineapple	Most any fern springeri fern banana yucca bird of paradise		

CHAPTER SIX

Secrets to a Beautiful Landscape

Do you remember the days when all they taught in school were the three R's, reading, 'riting, and 'rithmetic? Now, that's what I call getting down to the basics. I think more can be accomplished from study of the basics than anything else. So let's begin right now to simplify the whole thrust of landscape beautification to three simple basics, the three P's: *Planning, Planting,* and *Pruning.*

PLANNING THE LANDSCAPE

Completely planning your landscape before planting the first plant is very important. Don't be afraid of this step. Sure, you can't make a drawing as pretty as the pros, but with a few guidelines you can do an excellent job.

Begin by going to the middle of your front yard with a pencil and

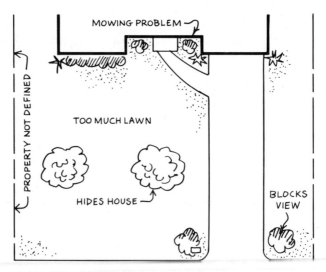

BEFORE (NO DESIGN)

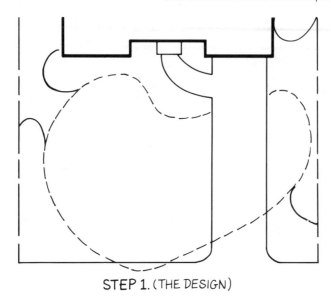

STEP 1. (THE DESIGN)

paper and look around. How do you feel – nervously exposed? Do you feel more a part of the road than your home? Most people would. The best way to unify all your property is with a sweeping curve that starts on the left and swings like a dizzy horseshoe around to the right.

Now, as shown in Step One, sketch your property and draw the sweeping line that marks the outline of your beds. Strive to reduce the actual grass area to cover only fifty percent of the front yard. This grass reduction along with keeping all plants confined to plant beds, greatly reduces mowing and lawn maintenance.

On your plan, draw an asterisk in the larger areas of the bed to show where you will locate trees and large accent plants – most homes will require six or eight. Your shrub row (whether hedge type or color shrubs) can be planted next to the house and to the rear of each bed to form a barrier for privacy. Mass the rest of the bed space with a low-growing ground cover.

Use only one variety of shrub and one variety of ground cover in each bed to keep the design appealing.

Where the bed sweeps across in front of the foot traffic flow, simply place stepping stones in the bed. Plants should never interfere with the movement of people in the landscape.

There, you see, landscaping is a simple three-step process.

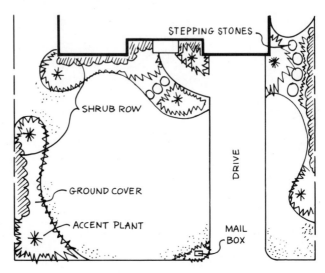

STEPPING STONES

SHRUB ROW

GROUND COVER

ACCENT PLANT

DRIVE

MAIL BOX

STEP 2. (PLACE PLANTS)

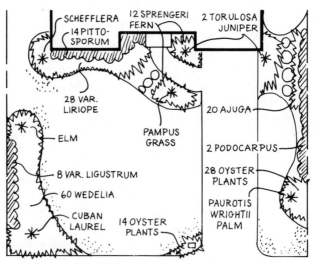

SCHEFFLERA
14 PITTO-SPORUM

12 SPRENGERI FERN

2 TORULOSA JUNIPER

28 VAR. LIRIOPE

20 AJUGA

ELM

PAMPUS GRASS

2 PODOCARPUS

8 VAR. LIGUSTRUM

28 OYSTER PLANTS

60 WEDELIA

CUBAN LAUREL

14 OYSTER PLANTS

PAUROTIS WRIGHTII PALM

STEP 3. (CHOOSE PLANTS)

Step One: Draw a sweeping curve around your entire front lawn. Don't get too fancy. Keep it simple and flowing.

Step Two: Arrange each bed with accent plants, palm or tree, plus a shrub row, and a mass of ground cover. Remember, use only one variety of each. Too many varieties in a bed cause visual chaos. Add stepping stones where bed crosses foot traffic flow.

Step Three: Choose plants and quantity. Keep in mind how these plants affect each other in color and texture. Simplicity is the key to aesthetic success.

Use the following symbols:

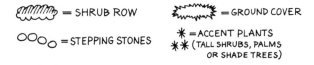

Now, that was all done rather quickly, so let's do it again with a differently shaped lot.

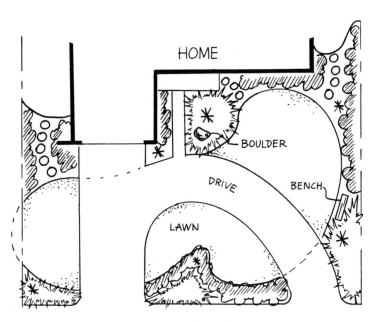

DIFFERENTLY SHAPED LOT

Once the flowing line is drawn in on your paper, mark the location of accent plants and trees with an asterisk. Next sketch in shrubs, ground covers, and stepping stones. Now, turn to the chapter entitled, Know Your Plants by Name. Look over the lists and make your choice of plants.

Most people begin their planning by thinking of plants. We can easily see now that the secret to landscape beautification begins with a study of line flow, foot traffic, and placement of plant types (accent plants, trees, shrubs, ground covers). Only after this has been completed do you sit down and determine which plants to use. This approach keeps the designing phase from becoming thought-cluttered.

The front of your property is often thought of as the main beauty spot; the sides and rear are more for functional use.

Most homes are built with one utility side. Located here are a door to the garage, water, gas, and electric meters, garden hose, trash can, etc. The other side is reserved for beauty. Here we find only windows.

The beauty side of the house should be developed into a landscaped

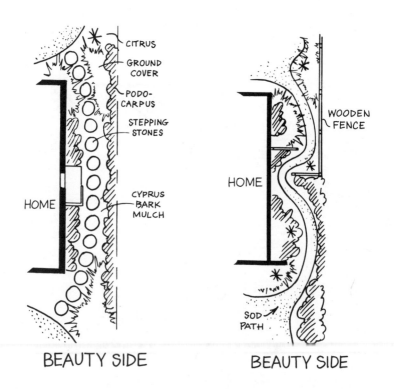

CITRUS
GROUND COVER
PODO-CARPUS
STEPPING STONES
CYPRUS BARK MULCH

HOME

BEAUTY SIDE

WOODEN FENCE

HOME

SOD PATH

BEAUTY SIDE

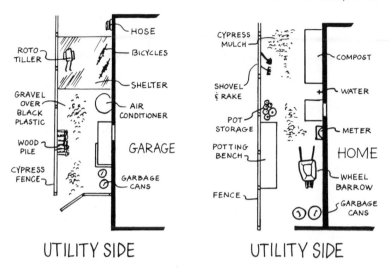

UTILITY SIDE   UTILITY SIDE

path to lead your guests to the backyard. Use fences, barrier plants, stepping stones, ground covers, arbors, or whatever is pleasant.

On the utility side, locate your sailboat, bicycles, pogo stick, wood pile, compost, garden tractor, and other assorted paraphernalia. It might be a good idea to fence in this area to hide the storage eyesore.

The backyard is often divided into at least two major areas. The first one your guest enters from the beauty side of the house is the privacy area. Locate here colorful shrubs, pleasant trees, patio, tiki hut, barbeque, wooden bench, hammock, swimming pool, putting green, or other pretty things. In the opposite end of the yard use more utility items,

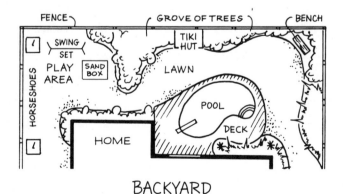

BACKYARD

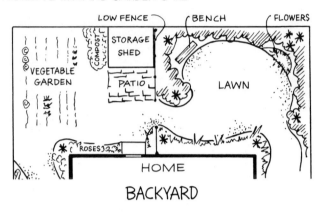

BACKYARD

such as sandbox, horseshoes, play yard with swing set, vegetable garden, garden for roses or other cut flowers, your storage shed, plant propagation bench, greenhouse, clothesline, etc.

These two rooms in the landscape must be divided by some type of barrier such as a low fence, hedge, or grove of trees. Following are two examples of landscaped backyards:

Planning your landscape on paper first is a must if you want to insure both utility and beauty. Here, you have been given some brief essentials to achieve a useful, attractive landscape around your home. If you want a thorough explanation on the entire landscape planning project written for the everyday homeowner, be sure to get a copy of my book, *Landscape Your Florida Home.*

PLANTING THE LANDSCAPE

It has been said it is better to plant a one-dollar plant in a three-dollar hole than a three-dollar plant in a one-dollar hole (old Chinese proverb). And that is what planting is all about. Keep reading.

Preparing to Plant

With the plan finished, your next step is to get a bag of flour and pour a white line on the lawn to correspond with the bed lines on your drawing. This procedure transfers the plan from your paper to your yard. Now, you have two choices: hand dig all the grass out of the plant beds (not recommended) or go to your nearest rental store and rent a sod cutter for half a day. With this machine you can quickly remove (but not easily, ladies) all the sod from the beds leaving a clean, sharp grass line at the edge. The removed sod can be piled in a compost pile.

With your plant beds shaped, you must concentrate on selecting the plants from your plant list and planting them. Take your plant list to a local nursery and ask to see the plants as well as any substitute the nurseryman may wish to suggest. Considering economics as well as immediate beauty, I would advise you to buy trees in a lerio can (10- to 15-gallon container), and accent plants in the 3-gallon size. Buy shrubs and hedge plants in the one-gallon size, and ground covers – which you will need a lot of – in a 4-inch pot or quart container. Ball-and-burlap plants are usually not as healthy as container plants. They shock too easily.

Once you get the plants home, set them all out where they are to be planted. Do this before digging the first hole. Look at the whole landscape and imagine the plants as they will appear at maturity. Are they well spaced? Most shrubs should be three feet apart and two feet away from the house foundation. Ground covers are usually closer together – one to two feet. Be sure to keep them at least eighteen inches from the front of the bed (the grass line).

How to Plant a Plant

To begin planting, dig the first hole with straight, vertical walls and a flat bottom. The hole should be at least eight inches wider than the plant container and eight inches deeper. Fill the bottom of the hole with a soil mix made by mixing one-third peat moss and two-thirds the soil taken from the hole and a double handful of cow manure.

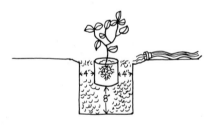

Now, remove the plant from the container by turning it upside down. Tap the container rim on a solid surface such as the edge of a low wall. If the plant does not come out, cut the container away with a pair of tin snips. Leaving the root ball intact, set the plant in the hole so that the top of the root mass is level with the surface of the ground. *Never plant a plant deeper than this.* Be sure to face the plant. Every shrub has a good side and a bad side. Face plants the way they look best.

When this is done, fill in the rest of the hole with the same mixture used in the bottom of the hole. The cow manure or any natural organic fertilizer is much better than a chemical fertilizer during this planting stage. After setting the plant, turn your shovel upside down and tamp the soil firm around the root ball. Build a small basin around the plant to collect and hold water. Lay a hose down over the rim of the basin and allow a slow flow to water your plant while you prepare the next hole.

Continue this method until all plants are planted and watered. Then, hand rake the bed to get the surface smooth. This is best done by turning your rake over so the teeth point up.

Staking Larger Plants

If any tree needs staking, do it immediately after planting. Tie a loop of a sturdy rope or cable around the trunk above the lowest limb. Be sure the loop is encased in a short tube cut from an old garden hose to prevent cutting through the trunk bark. Repeat this until you have three ties to support your tree. Don't pull the ties too tight. Remember, the tree wants to grow. Just make them snug. Then, as the wind blows, the root system and lower trunk will remain rigid, allowing new roots to take hold.

SNUG, NOT
TOO TIGHT

It is usually a good idea to stake smaller, single-trunk plants also. Use a garden stake one inch square and five feet long. Drive this stake alongside your plant, being careful not to damage the root system. Then, simply secure the trunk of the plant to the stake with a soft string, a section of pantyhose, or strips of cloth. Be sure to use something soft to prevent damaging the bark along the trunk. Tie firmly but not too tightly.

Which Mulch to Use

The final step in planting is to mulch your newly planted beds. Here is a list of many mulches commonly used in Florida:

1. Shredded Cypress Bark: One of the best mulches because the shreds interlock preventing wash-away during heavy rainfall. It also keeps its rich red-brown color longer than most organic mulches. Always buy the better grade, 100% bark, commonly called type A. The cheaper type B (half bark and half wood) just isn't worth it. It turns gray and floats away during heavy rains.

2. Sawdust: Excellent where a soft mulch is required but blows away during dry windy days and decomposes rapidly, requiring replacement often.

3. Pine Bark Nuggets: A rich looking mulch used on flat beds where it does not wash away during a heavy rain. If exposed to sunlight it bleaches gray and loses its eye appeal.

4. Cocoa Bean Hulls: Where available, these gems create a bold contrast because of their deep, rich, brown color.

5. Rocks: Common where a strong contrast is desired or around pools where organic mulch particles tend to blow in the water. Available in small, medium, and large size in brown or white colors. The cheaper limestone reduces the soil acidity and may become hazardous to plants. Rock mulches do not offer the warm, natural appearance available from the organic mulches and should be used sparingly in the landscape.

6. Pine Needles: An excellent mulch for several reasons: it holds its color, allows soil surface to receive plenty of air and, perhaps most importantly, it is usually free for the taking.

7. Black Plastic: Many people put flexible black plastic (polyethylene) over a plant bed just before mulching to keep weeds from growing. This practice becomes hazardous to the plants during the rainy season when excess water can't evaporate from the soil surface. It is just as hazardous during the drought season when it becomes difficult for water to get to the roots. If you feel you must cover the ground with something because of a persistent weed problem, use several layers of newspaper covered with a bag of mulch to camouflage it. The newspaper will remain damp, allow moisture penetration and evaporation, and will keep out most weeds. In a year or two the newspaper will decompose to further enrich the soil. By then you will have halted the weed problem and it is unlikely that it will return.

Why Mulch?

Mulching Florida soils is highly recommended because:
1. It helps retain moisture in a normally sandy and well drained soil.
2. It keeps the soil surface cooler allowing healthy growth.
3. It warms the soil in winter preventing root damage from cold.

4. It enhances landscape beauty by punctuating shapes of beds.
5. It aids in weed control.
6. It aids in nematode control by building up natural fungus enemies.
7. It prevents soil erosion during rainy periods.
8. It reduces surface erosion due to strong winds in dry, windy seasons.

PRUNING THE LANDSCAPE

Herein lies the real secret to landscape beautification – pruning. I have designed and installed hundreds of landscapes for various clients often to return in a year or two and find the project neglected and in chaos. Not to follow up on a beautification project leads to worse results than not to have started. Pruning is an important job and should not be taken lightly.

Why Prune?

There are four reasons why we prune plants:
1. To improve health by cutting out diseased or damaged plant parts.
2. To control size and shape.
3. To increase flower display. Pruning terminal branches stimulates side shoots with numerous but small flowers. Pruning side shoots (disbudding) channels energy into the terminal branch to produce a single but large flower.
4. To thicken or thin the mass of a plant.

Pruning Tools

Dozens of assorted pruning utensils and pieces of equipment exist, but the home grounds-keeper needs only four basic tools to solve his pruning problems:

1. Shears are common. This tool is almost exclusively used for trimming hedges. Don't let temptation encourage you to twist the handles and tear loose a stubborn twig. The electric shears are fast replacing the hand shears in popularity.

2. Pruning Snips or hand pruners are the handiest of all pruning tools. They are used to clip off twigs up to finger size.

3. Loppers are used to lop off limbs up to one inch in diameter. These are most often used in conjunction with an extension pole to reach tree tops.

4. Pruning Saws easily remove larger limbs. Many pruning saws are curved and have cutting teeth faced in the opposite direction than that of a carpenter's saw. This makes sawing easier when you're standing on a limb or ladder. Cross-cut saws are quite popular these days.

When to Prune

Perhaps the most often asked question is, "When am I supposed to prune my _____?"

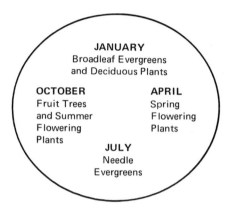

Let's begin the year with January. If broadleaf evergreens are pruned late in the year, they may not have enough growing season left to flush out new leaves and will look chopped up all during the winter. Prune them in January. If deciduous plants are pruned in warm months, they often bleed or ooze sap that attracts insects and creates an unsightly trunk. Prune these also in mid-winter

The next pruning season, April, includes azaleas, camellias, and a large assortment of spring flowering plants. Pruning should not begin until after the flowers fall and new growth begins late in the spring. If pruning is done during the fall or winter you may cut off the buds that have developed for next year's flowers. If pruned in the summer, you may encounter the broadleaf evergreen problem stated above.

Summer, or July, is the time to prune needle evergreens. A late summer flush of growth will cover pruned limb scars. Young pines are pruned by removing 50% of the candle that has flushed out since spring.

The last pruning should commence in the fall after all summer flowers have fallen and fruit has matured and been harvested. For plants that bear year-round, such as citrus, I have found that pruning during the flowering season in early spring works best. Most citrus will produce twice as many flowers as necessary and will drop many of these flowers or young fruit before they reach half-size. If you prune during this season, the tree will tend to hold most all of the flowers left intact, providing an average crop.

Eleven Pruning Tips

1. Aim buds by pruning just above a bud that is aimed at a hollow spot in the shrub mass. The new limb growing from this bud will fill that hollow spot.

2. Remove seed pods after flowers fade. Many flowering plants, such as marigolds and crape myrtle, will produce more flowers, and often a second crop.

3. Water sprouts often appear on citrus during the rainy season. These are new shoots that grow rapidly several feet beyond the normal tree spread and have extra large leaves. Cut off 50% of these freak shoots bringing them back in line with the leaf mass.

4. Root suckers growing around the base of a tree should be pruned off.

5. Remove all suckers that grow below a grafted area. These are a wild variety and will not produce desirable flowers or fruit.

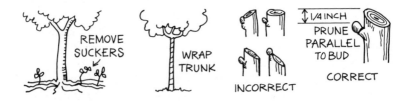

6. Wrap trunks of deciduous trees when they are transplanted into full sun. Otherwise, they are likely to get sun-scald.

7. Apical dominance means a pruned plant will produce 90% of its new growth on the ends where the cut was made. So, if you want new shoots at the bottom of a shrub you must cut the shrub back 50% or more.

8. Prune young limbs at an angle parallel to the bud. This cut should be about ¼ inch above the bud.

9. Nubs of limbs should never be left. They will rot and rarely heal. Make all large cuts flush with the trunk. In this manner they will heal over with new bark in one year's time.

10. When removing large limbs always make three cuts. The first one cuts through the bark several inches from the trunk. The second one cuts off the limb a foot from the trunk. The third one cuts off the nub. This technique prevents a heavy limb from tearing the bark down the side of the trunk, causing an open wound.

11. All wounds from cut limbs of one-inch diameter or larger should be painted with pruning paint. Don't use house paints.

Five Tips for Plant Surgery

When plants have been poorly maintained, incorrectly pruned, have undesirable shapes or receive damage from inclement weather, plant surgery becomes necessary.

1. Trees that fork close to the ground should have their crotch strengthened to prevent strong winds from splitting the tree in half. Use a ¾-inch rod inserted through drilled holes. Wire wrapped around the limbs will eventually choke the trunk.

2. A hollow trunk in a decayed tree can be strengthened by crossing rods through the trunk after removing all dead wood and painting decayed area with a copper fungicide and pruning paint.

3. Ragged cuts on a tree trunk should have bark cut away in the shape of a football to facilitate callusing and rapid healing.

4. Fill dirt is often brought in to raise the soil level of a home site. This can kill trees, especially pines. Build a rock bank to keep soil three feet away from tree trunk and place tile pipe vertically every ten feet over root system to provide aeration to the roots.

BEFORE   AFTER   FILL DIRT PROTECTION   ½ INCH
                                                         FOR
                                                         DRAINAGE

5. Concrete should not be used to fill rotted pockets in tree trunks. After you chase out the neighborhood squirrels and steal their nuts, remove all decay and drill a half-inch hole up into the bottom of the pocket to provide drainage. Paint the entire pocket with a copper fungicide and pruning paint including the newly drilled hole. Concrete traps moisture that initiates decay. If structural support becomes necessary, drill a half-inch hole and bolt a threaded rod in place.

The secrets to a beautiful landscape are first to make a complete landscape plan showing locations of flowing beds, accent plants, trees, shrubs, and ground covers; and then to install the plants following the principles in this chapter. Finally, landscape plants must be maintained on a sound yearly basis. This maintenance includes pruning as well as mulching, fertilizing, watering, and spraying for insects, diseases, and weeds. If any one of these areas is lacking in your landscape beautification project, you are doomed to failure.

Gardeners alleged to be green-thumbers maintain a sound program as outlined above. Their secret is not so much in years of experience as it is in following a sound, basic program.

CHAPTER SEVEN

Secrets to a Perfect Lawn

Grass is still the most popular ground cover in Florida because:
1. It covers a large area quickly.
2. The cost is comparatively inexpensive.
3. The maintenance, often, is lower.
4. It withstands heavy foot traffic.
5. It controls erosion.
6. Grass is aesthetically appealing as compared to grass substitutes.
7. It "cools" the landscape.

We have several ravishing varieties in Florida that come in three dazzling colors: green, yellow, and brown. I have seen some lawns go through all three color changes in one season. St. Augustine and Bahia lead the popularity pack for the greens.

The lawn grass best adapted to your location and the one that does not make excessive demands on your time and budget is the best grass for you.

Most of the grasses growing this far south thrive year-round and require more fertilizing, mowing, edging, and spraying than we are accustomed to up north. Another big difference in Florida lawns is that most of the grasses are applied by sod instead of seed, and always one hundred percent of one variety, instead of a mixture of varieties. Seeding is restricted to the season when both the night air and the ground are warm. This ranges from May to September in Central Florida, from June to September in North Florida, and from March to October in South Florida.

Before choosing your grass consider:
1. How much foot traffic the lawn may bear.
2. How much of the area is exposed to salt spray and shade.
3. The initial cost.
4. The yearly cost in dollars and hours required for maintenance.

77

SEVEN GOOD GRASSES

1. Bahia: The Argentine variety is perhaps the best all around-grass for the home lawn. Seed should be sown at 10 lbs. per 1000 sq. ft. and covered with ¼ inch of soil or sand and kept moist. Sodding is the most popular method of establishment but costs more.

The Pensacola variety is less expensive and often used as a pasture grass. It is sown at 5 lbs. per 1000 sq. ft. This variety sends up tall seed spikes making it unpopular as a lawn grass.

Bahia develops a deep root system on sandy soils enabling it to withstand drought conditions. However, it also grows quite well on poorly drained soils.

Argentine Bahia is a medium textured grass that prefers an acid soil.

Fertilize in the spring and fall with a 100 percent organic 6-6-6 at 25 lbs. per 1000 sq. ft. Bahia does poorly under conditions of heavy shade, salt air, and turns brown with the first film of frost.

Mowing should be done every week during the summer and fall. Mowing height is 2½ inches. Be sure to have mower blades sharpened each winter.

If your Bahia shrivels up like brown straw during a drought, don't get excited and unscrew the neighborhood fire hydrant. The blades have merely folded up to keep the hot sun from draining the last traces of stored moisture. This process is a self-preservation mechanism of the grass. To you, it is an indication to start watering. If watering is not possible (due to one of several reasons: water ban, too costly, you're away on vacation, you simply don't care, etc.) then keep calm and collected; the grass will survive serveral days in this condition. And sooner or later it is going to rain.

Watering should be done twice a week, preferably between sunup and noon so blades will dry well before nightfall, applying ¾ inches of water each time. How much is ¾ inches? Place a pie tin on the lawn in the area being sprinkled. Mark the time. When it is filled with ¾ inches of water, mark the time again. The time lapsed is how long you should water. This time will vary accoarding to water pressure, type of sprinkler, hose size, and volume capacity of your water system.

Power rake (or hand rake if you have a strong back and an empty pocketbook) your Bahia in early spring just prior to fertilizing to clean it and stimulate new growth. Raking is not necessary in fall. Most homeowners hire a lawn maintenance firm to power rake. Newly sodded lawns should not be raked the first spring.

It is wise to *catch grass clippings* when mowing to prevent thatch buildup. Excess thatch provides a haven for insects and diseases. Clippings can be thrown on the compost pile. If used as mulch, mix clipping with larger materials (leaves, pine needles, shredded cypress bark) to prevent matting.

Sound like a lot of work? Actually these are guidelines to prevent excess work. Bahia is a tough grass, that can withstand heavy foot traffic and is an excellent choice. But here is the key to keeping it thick: *Sow additional seed at 3 lbs. per 1000 sq. ft. each spring after raking. Then fertilize.*

2. St. Augustine: For many years St. Augustine has been the standard for Florida lawns because of its versatility. Floratam is a popular variety. Seville, a newer dwarf variety, is showing well. Bitter Blue, Floratine, and Common are also good varieties for the home grounds.

All St. Augustines have very wide blades and are vigorous growers. They should be *mowed* weekly at 2 inches (this height is important), and be sure to catch grass clippings. *Fertilize* in the spring, late summer, and early winter with 100 percent organic 6-6-6 at 25 lbs. per 1000 sq. ft. It grows on a wide range of soils including salty environments and heavy shade. St. Augustine is not available in seed and must be sodded or sprigged. Sprigging is an inexpensive method many find satisfactory.

To *sprig* a lawn, simply cut and dig sprigs from the runners of an established lawn and plant them about one foot apart in the new, smoothly raked area. A little fertilizer and water will help get them over the shock and off to a running start. Soon the sprigs will start to run and in about one year you'll have an established lawn.

Water St. Augustine a little more frequently than Bahia, about three times a week, putting on ¾ inches each time.

Have your St. Augustine lawn *Verticut* in the spring every three to five years. This is more costly than power raking Bahia, but will keep the runners from becoming so long they trip you. The practice of an occasional close mowing or scalping along with the regular mowing program to reduce build-up of vegetative top growth is advisable with St. Augustine as well as centipede and carpet grass. This technique may be done two to three times during the season of rapid growth.

St. Augustine is also a tough grass that wears well but will not withstand dry weather like Bahia. It grows much thicker than Bahia.

3. Zoysia: Zoysia is one of my favorites. It has many characteristics similar to St. Augustine but looks entirely different. The tiny blades make a fine-textured mat on the lawn resembling a carpet. Like St.

Augustine, zoysia withstands shaded areas and salty spray. Growing best on heavier soils that hold water, it does not tolerate drought and should be *watered* every other day.

Fertilize every three months with 100 percent organic 6-6-6 at 25 lbs. per 1000 sq. ft. of lawn. *Mow* with a reel mower (not a rotary type) every week or two leaving the blades about ¾ of an inch tall.

Zoysia grows slowly, wears well, and withstands frost. Although it may turn brown from frost, this doesn't seem to harm it.

When establishing a new lawn, zoysia must be sodded or plugged. Plugging is done by cutting two-inch squares from a piece of sod and planting them every eight inches.

4. Bermuda: There are two types of Bermuda grass, the seeded kind and the improved kind. The latter is always sodded since these hybrids do not produce seed. Seeded Bermuda, also called common or native Bermuda, is seldom seen as lawn grass in Florida. It frequently intrudes lawns as a weed.

There are several improved varieties, most of which are used on golf courses where very high maintenance is tolerated.

The improved variety most often used on home lawns is Ormond Bermuda or Tifway. From a distance they look much like zoysia, but unlike the stiff blades of zoysia, Bermuda is very soft to the touch. This characteristic affords comfort to the barefoot gardener.

Bermuda, being the highest quality of all grasses, has the highest maintenance. It must be *mowed* with a reel mower about every three days. Mow to a height of ¾ of an inch.

Fertilize every other month with 100 percent organic 6-6-6 at 25 lbs. per 1000 sq. ft. Extra doses of a nitrogen fertilizer from time to time will be beneficial. Golf courses use ammonium nitrate.

If these grasses are mowed too infrequently or with a rotary mower, they will turn brown for several days.

Bermuda does not withstand shade or beach salt and suffers under drought conditions. *Water* every other day. The wear to foot traffic is good and the growth rate is very fast.

Because Bermuda makes such a dense mat, golf courses aerate the turf from time to time. Bermuda is the most beautiful lawn, but you must know how to care for it.

5. Centipede: About the lowest maintenance grass, centipede is medium in texture, requires *fertilizing* only once a year, preferably in the spring, and is *mowed* to 1½ inches only twice a month.

Acid soils are preferred as is full sun or at least filtered sunlight. Wear is poor, so don't use it where the kids play ball. Neither is it good for salty beach conditions. *Water* once a week. Frost will harm the grass if used in North Florida. Rarely is it grown in South Florida.

Centipede is established by seed or sod and would make a good lawn grass where the above conditions prevail if it were not for a tiny insect called ground pearl that notoriously destroys these lawns. A good control is not available.

6. Carpet Grass: This is a native plant that often creeps into Bahia lawns as a weed. If seeded or sodded where wet, poorly drained acid soils exist, it will thrive better than most grasses. Otherwise, it will have to be *watered* often.

The maintenance is low. *Mow* twice a month to keep down the seed spikes, and *fertilize* just once a year. Mowing height is 1½ inches. Carpet grass tolerates partial shade but does not endure salt spray, drought, frost, or heavy foot traffic.

7. Temporary Grasses: Occasionally an overseeding of a winter grass is beneficial to green the lawn after a frost browns your permanent grass. Redtop, bluegrass, and Kentucky fescue have been used, but rye seems to be the most popular.

Italian rye forms a dense root system that will hinder the recovery of your permanent grass, so sow it sparingly, about three pounds per 1000 sq. ft. Fertilize in the fall and winter for a beautiful, green cover. You can expect it to die in the early summer heat.

As beautiful as Florida lawns are they have their problems too, namely insects and diseases. *Why do we have so many lawn insects in Florida?* The same reason we have so many people – nice weather. The insects found this out many years ago and people are now just catching on. With the warm winters these little critters don't bother to die out for the cold season the way they do up north. Instead, they continue to feed and reproduce.

Why do we have so many lawn diseases in Florida? Mostly because of the high humidity and frequency at which people water their lawn. Remember, those tiny pathogens that cause diseases require moisture to reproduce. Water your lawn early in the day so the sun will dry the surface before nightfall.

Now look over the following list and see if something looks familiar.

TEN COMMON LAWN INSECTS

1. Mole Crickets: One of the greatest problems affecting all of the lawn grasses commonly grown in Florida, particularly Bahia and Bermuda. These 1½-inch crickets with short, fat, front legs adapted for digging are most active in the late summer and early spring. As they

burrow just under the soil surface cutting off roots, they cause the soil to feel spongy under foot. Control is achieved by repeated applications of dursban or diazinon or by having lawn professionally treated.

2. Chinch Bugs: They are a major problem in most all St. Augustine lawns. These oval-shaped insects, less than ¼ inch long, have a white marking on their backs resembling an "x," or a white band running from side to side. As they suck juice from the blades the grass appears brown, usually in patches with yellowish margins. Numerous chemicals on the market will control them, but the secret is to spray every two months during the summer and fall. An inexpensive hose-end sprayer works well. Chinch bugs rarely affect other grasses.

3. Sod Webworms: These light-colored caterpillars, about ¾ inches long, chew grass blades at night. Upon close examination you will see these chewed blades in dying areas of the lawn. The adult moth, also about ¾ inches long, will fly from the grass as you walk across it, only to light about five feet away. Do not confuse these adults with the smaller leaf hoppers. Most damage is done during the hot, dry season and occurs on all grass varieties. Sevin or diazinon is a safe effective control.

4. White Grubs: Light-colored, c-shaped caterpillars with a dark rear end and a reddish brown front end can be found as you dig in most any soil that contains grass roots. If you dig up several in a small area then soil should be drenched with Sevin or a suitable insecticide. A few white grubs do little damage and should be ignored.

5. Rhinoceros Beetles: This beautiful creature (depending on how you look at him) actually causes minimum damage. But the white grubs hatched from the eggs may be a problem. Many homeowners find a deep hole in their lawn wide enough to drop in a half dollar. A mound of dirt usually accompanies the hole. Pour a solution of Sevin into the hole, and you will eliminate this problem. The male beetle has three horns, the female has none. Both are hard and shiny brown. Other names for this creature are ox bettle and elephant beetle.

6. Army Worms: Found feeding in all lawns, these large caterpillars have a white streak up their backs ending in an inverted "V" on their

WHITE GRUB   RHINOCEROS BEETLE   ARMYWORM   SCALES

head. In platoons they march like an army across the lawn, devouring as they go. The grass blades appear ragged and chewed; often not in definite patches like that of sod webworms. Control with Sevin or some other suitable chemical. A smaller, striped caterpillar, the grass looper, may be found in taller grasses. These move like a little measuring worm. Control in the same manner.

7. Scales: Grass scales, such as Rhodesgrass scale and Bermuda-grass scale, cause infested areas to thin out and turn yellow. Grass may die if insect is not controlled with malathion. These juice suckers are very tiny and appear as small bumps at the base of the blade. They may have a cottony mass over them.

8. Leafhoppers: There are many species of leafhoppers, rarely exceeding ¼-inch in length. All are slender and either hop or fly as you walk through the grass. Leafhoppers suck plant juices, leaving tiny spots on the blade surface. They also aid in the spread of disease. Control with malathion.

9. Billbugs: These weevils, about ⅜ of an inch long, use their snout to chew grass roots, especially on zoysia and Bermuda lawns. The grub is white, about the same length, and also feeds on roots. Grass is usually killed in irregular patches. Baygon is a good control if drenched on a wet lawn.

10. Spittlebugs: A frothy spittle at the base of grass blades indicates the nesting place of young spittlebugs. The adults, brown with two orange bands across their back, can be very damaging to grass at times. Mature insects are about one-half inch long. Spray with diazinon or malathion if population becomes large.

LEAFHOPPER   BILLBUG

SPITTLEBUG AND NEST

The following chart will be useful in tracking down the culprit ruining your lawn's appearance.

PERFORM THESE TESTS TO DETERMINE WHICH
INSECT IS AFFECTING YOUR LAWN

1. Ground under lawn feels spongy.	**Mole Crickets**
2. Brown areas in St. Augustine during warm weather. "X" marked insects ¼ inch long seen.	**Chinch Bugs**
3. Grass blades chewed away.	**Sod Webworms**
4. White grubs found under declining sod.	**White Grubs**
5. One-inch diameter hole neatly dug in lawn.	**Rhinoceros Beetles**
6. Many large caterpillars seen feeding on grass blades in fall.	**Armyworms**
7. Areas in lawn yellowing and thinning out.	**Scales**
8. Tiny spots seen on blades in weak areas of the lawn.	**Leafhoppers**
9. Small weevils seen in weak areas of the lawn.	**Bill bugs**
10. Frothy spittle seen at the base of grass blades	**Spittlebugs**

TEN COMMON LAWN DISEASES

1. Brown Patch: Perhaps the most common disease attacking all varieties of lawns, brown patch appears as small or large, round or irregular brown areas. Often the base of the leaf blade rots and can be pulled apart from the roots. The best symptom is the appearance of seemingly unaffected blades of grass growing within the brown, dying area. The disease is most prevalent when temperature is between 80° and 90° F. The chemicals Daconil 2787, dithane M-45 (Fore), and PCNB (Terraclor) all provide good control. Water only once a week when lawn is diseased. Spray weekly for a month.

2. Dollar Spot: Especially common on Bermuda, bahia, and zoysia, this fungus leaves solid brown patches a few inches in diameter in the lawn. These spots occur mostly in the spring and fall months, especially during a drought spell. Control by spraying Daconil 2787 or dithane M-45 (Fore) and fertilizing with a high nitrogen fertilizer. Do not confuse

BROWN PATCH

BROWN PATCH
LEAF BLADE

DOLLAR SPOT

dollar spot with damage caused by dog urine or a gasoline or mineral spirits spill; all have similar symptoms.

3. Gray Leafspot: Found primarily on St. Augustine, this disease causes oval or round spots to appear on the grass blades. These spots have a tan center with a dark halo. The fungus is spread by frequent watering and by use of a high nitrogen fertilizer. Besides cutting back these two activities most any turf fungicide (Daconil 2787, Fore, thiram) will prove beneficial.

4. Melting Out: Sometimes called *helminthosporum*, it is usually easy to recognize. Look for tiny, purplish-brown specks on the blades of Bermuda, St. Augustine, or ryegrass in areas of the lawn that turn reddish-brown and die. Grass blades may appear bright yellow in advanced stages. Damage is most severe during spring and fall months. Spray Daconil 2787 or Fore if disease persists.

5. Cottony Blight: Here, we have another lawn-loser. Some call it *Pythium*. This blight has cottony spots that appear as a late symptom. Early symptoms are spots several inches in diameter where the grass is blackened and water-soaked or matted together. Soon the lawn appears brown with a slight reddish tinge. Maximum damage occurs to Bermuda and ryegrass during rainy months or periods of frequent irrigation, especially when temperature is 90° to 95° F.

Sprays of Subdue repeated weekly during the hot, wet season often prove beneficial. Curtailing mowing and watering during periods of disease activity also help reduce this hard to control lawn disease.

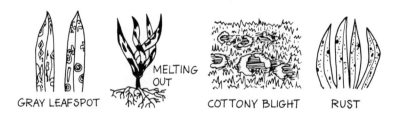

GRAY LEAFSPOT   MELTING OUT   COTTONY BLIGHT   RUST

6. Rust: Attacks ryegrass and zoysia during mild to warm, humid weather. It is occasionally found on St. Augustine and Bermuda. Lawns appear thin and unhealthy. Tiny orange pustules on the grass blades rub off on your finger. To control, reduce watering frequency and spray with zineb, Fore, or sulfur.

7. Fairy Ring: Perhaps you remember this one from your youth. A large, dark green ring appears in the lawn. In the ring is a series of mushrooms (under which live the elves of fairy-tale land). These mushrooms usually appear after a heavy rain. The fungus can be active, however, without the presence of mushrooms. Since control is difficult, an increased watering and fertilizing program usually proves sufficient in home lawns.

FAIRY RING

SLIME MOLD

NEMATODES

8. Slime Mold: If your lawn appears to be covered with soot, it is probably slime mold. A light or dark gray substance covers the blades and can be easily swept off with a broom or washed away with a garden hose. Because the fungus does not directly affect the grass, no other control is needed.

9. Chlorosis: While this yellowing of the lawn is not caused by a disease pathogen, symptoms may appear so. If the soil pH is not correct; most lawns will become chlorotic (turn yellow). Chlorosis is usually caused by an iron deficiency. Apply iron sulfate at 10 lbs. per 1000 sq. ft.

10. Nematodes: Nematodes are one of the worst pests of home lawns. Nematodes are microscopic eelworms that feed on grass roots. If the lawn is declining, and none of the above maladies seem to be the problem, take a soil sample to your local Country Extension Office for a nematode test. A soil sample is one pint of soil collected from several locations in the lawn, six inches below the ground, and mixed together. If you do not wish to wait for test results, have your lawn treated by a certified pest control operator.

If the above list of ailments isn't enough to curdle your green cuticle, then note: Over one hundred diseases have been found on lawn grasses in Florida (fortunately most are rare) as well as hundreds of insects. But that is not all. Several larger pests do severe damage to home lawns including moles, pocket gophers (salamanders), and armadillos. I have found the best way to control these, other than by using baits or traps which seldom work, is to eliminate their food source.

Most of these animals are feeding on grubs or other root-chewers. By drenching an appropriate mixture of Sevin, diazinon, dursban, or other suitable insecticide you can eliminate these pests and the larger animals will go elsewhere in search of food.

Growing beautiful lawns in Florida is not difficult if you familiarize yourself with the ailments. You do, however, have an alternative with ground covers, brick, stone, artifical turf, sand, mulch, decking, outdoor carpet, and pine needles.

PERFORM THESE TESTS TO DETERMINE WHICH DISEASE
IS AFFECTING YOUR LAWN

1. Large brown patches seen that contain several healthy, green blades in the damaged area.   **Brown Patch**
2. Small brown spots, 2 to 3 inches in diameter seen in lawn.   **Dollar Spot**
3. Tan spots in grass blades of St. Augustine with darker halo around them.   **Gray Leaf Spot**
4. Tiny, purplish-brown spots on grass blades.   **Melting Out**
5. Grass blades matted together, cottony substance may be seen.   **Cottony Blight**
6. Orange spots seen on grass blades.   **Rust**
7. Mushrooms present in a circular pattern.   **Fairy Ring**
8. Grass covered with a sooty substance.   **Slime Mold**
9. Grass turning yellow throughout lawn.   **Chlorosis**
10. Lawn slowly declining, perks up temporarily when watered.   **Nematodes**

CHAPTER EIGHT
Eliminating Weeds and Poisonous Plants

Weeds cost the United States over five billion dollars each year in estimated annual losses. These losses are second only to those in the nation's agricultural economy caused by soil erosion. No wonder we are so concerned about control of these noxious pests.

There are three ways to control weeds in the home lawn:
1. CULTURAL—By starving the weeds through choice watering.
2. MECHANICAL—By digging or hand pulling.
3. CHEMICAL—By spraying herbicides.

Often it is a combination of all three of these and much patience that ultimately kills the weeds. One thing is sure. If you have a new lawn or a weed-free old lawn and *do not* practice some type of weed control, you are sure to acquire a selection of weeds within a few years. Weeds are ever-persistent in Florida. It is unfortunate, but many weeds come with the sod at purchase time. It is not practical for sod farmers to spray hundreds of acres for weeds. Thus, it becomes the homeowner's burden to eliminate the weeds.

Weeds have been defined as plants in the wrong place. Some weeds can be used as ground covers if they are planted thickly in an area where nothing else is growing. Some that have been used are artillery fern, creeping Charlie, purslane, and oxalis. But, scattered amongst your lawn grass, they become a weed and are sometimes tough to eliminate.

Because most of these weeds are shallow-rooted, deep watering your lawn aids in weed control. Deep watering simply means to water heavily but infrequently. It is the daily, light watering that keep moisture near the surface to feed the weeds. Infrequent watering allows the top few inches of your lawn to dry out, weakening the weeds as the deeper-rooted lawn grass drinks its fill a few feet down. To deep water your lawn, apply one inch of water once a week.

Before studying the simple control methods, let's become more familiar with weeds. The following lists some of the more common weeds found growing in home lawns.

LEARN THESE TEN COMMON WEEDS

1. Spotted Spurge: See how the small leaves grow from the stem in pairs? There is usually a reddish spot in the center of each leaf. Stems are hairy, spindly and may grow to one foot tall. Milky juice inside.

2. Creeping Charlie: Leaves are shaped similar to spurge only smaller. Stems creep along ground often under grass blades. Tiny flowers borne on three-inch stems are purple to white. Also called *Matchweed,* the distinguishing characteristic is the small teeth on each leaf that start at the center edge and continue to tip.

3. Pennywort: Leaves are about the size of a quarter with lobed margins. Plant creeps across lawns that are kept *too wet.* This plant loves poorly drained, overly irrigated areas. Dry the lawn surface by reducing the watering frequency. Also called *Dollarweed.*

4. Artillery Fern: Has tiny leaves that grow thick along the stems. Plants may be several inches tall. Is attractive if used as a ground cover in a shady spot. Likes damp locations, so reduce watering to starve it out.

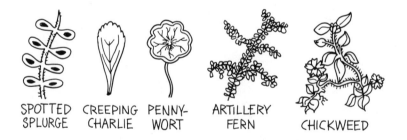

SPOTTED   CREEPING   PENNY-   ARTILLERY
SPLURGE   CHARLIE   WORT   FERN   CHICKWEED

5. Chickweed: Usually grows in the cooler winter months. Creeping plants several inches tall with tiny star-shaped, white flowers. May become thick in some locations. Easily hand-pulled but seeds come up the following year, thus it must be pulled before seeds are produced. Has hairy stems.

6. Grass Weeds: This listing is a catch-all group including such notorious weeds as: nutgrass, goosegrass, sandspur, wild Bermuda, and watergrass. Notice they all have blades instead of leaves. This makes

SANDSPUR

FLORIDA BETONY

selective, chemical control nearly impossible in lawn areas. Spot treatment is used.

7. Florida Betony: Plants grow yearly from white, ring-constricted tubers about two inches long. Oval leaves have toothed margin. These weeds may be a foot or more in height in flower beds. Tiny flowers are purple to white.

8. Florida Purslane: Also called pusley, this weed resembles chickweed but grows in summer. The tiny, white flowers have six petals. The weak stems are well branched. Common purslane has succulent, reddish stems that grow lower to the ground and much resembles portulaca (rose moss).

9. Creeping Beggarweed: Has a clover-like appearance but smaller leaves. This is a hard weed to control as it creeps along below your lawn mower blade. Tiny flowers are purplish. During dry periods, leaves fold up to protect themselves. The large-leaf variety has flat seeds that stick to clothing. These plants grow up to two or three feet in fields.

FLORIDA PURSLANE

CREEPING BEGGARWEED

NETTLE

10. Nettle: Not too common in home lawns but listed here because of its poisonous characteristics. The tiny hairs along the stem, if touched, will sting like a honeybee. Don't try to pull this one out, dig it. Reddening and swelling accompany the sting. Medication is of little use.

HOW TO CONTROL WEEDS

Chemical control of weeds is a complicated, often unrewarding endeavor. Chemical ingredients are frequently changed, making it difficult to recommend brands by trade names. The study of the following categories will, however, make chemical weed control a simple task. When buying herbicides (weed killers) be sure to ask for a product that contains the below-listed chemicals. Don't ask for the chemical itself. You may have to look on the label for the chemical name.

1. To kill leaf weeds without harming grass: The term selective chemical control applies when a herbicide, sprayed over a grass lawn containing broadleaf weeds, selectively kills the broadleafs without harming the grass. The most common selective chemicals to be found in garden shops today are dicamba, and 2,4-D. Look for these names on the label and follow the directions.

Both of these chemicals are translocative, meaning they should be applied to weed leaves. Here, they are absorbed and transported via the plant's vein system to the roots where they kill the weed. Thus, you should repeat the application if a rain washes off the herbicide within 24 hours after you spray. Translocative herbicides are slow-acting and may take a week or two before you notice any results.

Since several of these broadleaf weeds are persistent and tough to kill, you may have to spray three or four times at weekly intervals. Be careful not to let spray drift to nearby shrubs or flowers. These sprays have been found to harm St. Augustine lawns. A better chemical to use for selective control of broadleaf weeds in St. Augustine grass is atrazine.

2. To kill grass weeds without harming broadleaf plants: This situation exists where grass weeds are growing in a flower bed, shrub border, or under trees. The chemical dalapon is a good, selective grass killer. Like 2,4-D, it is a translocative herbicide. Common for cattail control.

3. To kill tops of plants without affecting soil: Soil is not affected when Roundup, or Phytar (cacodylic acid) is applied to the weeds. These herbicides simply burn the tops of the weeds without harming the soil. To stop them permanently, repeat applications periodically as weeds continue to emerge. Kills off all weeds growing under trees or tall shrubs without harming trunk or roots of the existing plants.

4. To kill all plants and the soil for several months: These chemicals are commonly used next to walks and drives or under fences where it is desired to kill all plant growth for a long time. Herbicides to look for are diuron (Karmex) or Pramitol.

5. To kill young plants without affecting mature ones: Simazine (80 WP) mixed at the rate of one pound to 20 gallons of water will treat an area 100 feet by 50 feet. This rate will help keep out new weeds in an established lawn or shrub border for one season.

6. To kill all plants, roots, and tops without permanently harming soil: The chemical vapam is used to sterilize soil. It kills everything: plants, weed seeds, disease pathogens. In a few weeks, the vapam will evaporate from the soil, leaving it free to be reseeded or planted. Vegetable growers often sterilize their soil with vapam prior to each planting season.

7. To kill germinating seeds as they blow in without harming existing plants: The chemicals Treflan (used in established shrubs and flowers), Balan (in established lawn), or Dacthal (in both) will kill young seedlings as they germinate without harming existing plants.

8. To kill poison ivy or other viney plants: Amitrole sprayed on the leaves of poison ivy will kill it without harming the trunks of large trees. This herbicide is absorbed into the system of all plants (grasses or broad-leafs) if applied to the leaves.

Many herbicides are hazardous to the skin and eyes. Always spray following label directions, wear gloves, a long-sleeve shirt buttoned at the collar, and spray only on calm days. Wash sprayer thoroughly after each use to prevent corrosion and mark the sprayer *Weed Killer.*

POISON PLANTS AROUND YOUR HOME

A surprisingly large number of plants used in and around the home are toxic if accidentally eaten. Others are irritating to the skin if touched. Normally, these plants would not be eaten but may be accidentally ingested by children. Pets have an instinct that often tells them what not to eat. Familarization with several of these more common species is wise.

Most poisonous plants have such an unpleasant taste that it is unlikely they would be chewed to any extent. A few, however, have desirable flavors. In most cases a physician can treat the symptoms and effectively reduce pain or nausea.

Children should be taught to avoid putting anything in their mouths except food.

Collecting and eating mushrooms, unless you know positively that they are edible, is a very dangerous business.

The following is a list of plants often found around the home. It does not include field or wood plants such as poison ivy, bracken fern, and rattle box which contain parts toxic to people and farm animals.

Learn These Ten Poisonous Plants

1. Yellow Allamanda: This common vine (or shrub, if pruned often), popular for its large, yellow flowers that bloom all through the warm months, is noted for being poisonous – especially the fruit. However, no known poison has been extracted.

2. Castor Bean: A vigorous, annual herb that grows to the size of a small tree. The robust stems may be green, red, or purple and hold large, starlike leaves with prominent veins. Castor bean contains a poisonous principal, ricin, as well as ricinoleic acid and oleic acid.

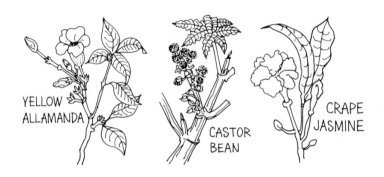

3. Crape Jasmine: A large, succulent shrub much resembling gardenia but with smaller flowers. The roots, bark, and fragrant flowers may be harmful if eaten.

4. Crown of Thorns: Quite common as a thorny, low-growing border plant, the pink to red flowers, although small, will bloom from spring through fall. Crown of thorns belongs to the Euphorbia family whose many species have all been branded as being poisonous because of an unclassified toxic substance in the milky sap.

5. Dieffenbachia: Often called "dumb cane," dieffenbachia is one

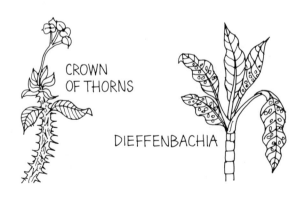

of the most common house plants used today in homes, offices, and shopping malls. The large, succulent leaves along canes two to six feet tall may be speckled or striped with colorful variegations. The juice contains calcium oxalate and, if ingested, causes swelling of the tongue that blocks breathing. A tiny dose may be fatal to small children or to cats who like to scratch things and lick their paws. Dieffenbachia is a good house plant, but be careful when you cut its cane for propagation. Wash all knives and bench tops that come into contact with the sap.

6. Gloriosa Lily: One of my favorites because of the delicate, fiery, yellow to red flowers that seem to hang upside down. Leaf tips have tendrils that cling to a support. All parts of gloriosa lily are highly poisonous, especially the tuberous roots. Symptoms include numbness of lips, tongue, and throat; nausea and diarrhea with blood; giddiness and loss of power in limbs; a quick feeble pulse; convulsions, and loss of consciousness.

GLORIOSA LILY

7. Angel's Trumpet: A spectacular flowering shrub whose kin make up the jimsonweed family, all of which are poisonous. All parts of these plants are poisonous, especially the seed. Children have been poisoned by eating the fruit or sucking the flowers. Large, white flowers hang down.

8. Mango: This plant may appear out of place here since mango fruits are sold on the roadside and in grocery stores. The tree is, however, a member of the poison family and susceptible people who contact any part of the plant may develop a dermatitis similar to poison ivy. If you've never tried this delicious fruit, eat just one small bite to note if any irritation of the mouth occurs. Few people are affected, and cooking destroys the causal material.

9. Pencil Cactus: Also called milkbush and seldom grown outdoors

ANGEL'S TRUMPET

MANGO

in North Florida, this curiosity plant contains a toxic material that has been used as a fish poison in its native India. Handling causes no problem.

10. Oleander: One of the most popular coastal shrubs in Florida because of its high salt resistance and many months of showy flowers. The flowers vary from white through pink and red. All parts of this plant are deadly poisonous if eaten. Toxic effects have occurred in individuals cooking hot dogs on an oleander stick or inhaling smoke from burning twigs.

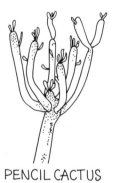
PENCIL CACTUS

OLEANDER

If poisoning is suspected from eating or handling any poisonous plant, contact your nearest poison control center and your physician. Whenever possible, always take along the plant specimen suspected to be toxic.

Numerous other plants in the Florida landscape contain poison materials, but these plants need not be eradicated from your lawn. They are commonly grown by thousands of homeowners. Just remember the rule: "Touch but don't eat."

Before proceeding, take a moment to look up the number of the poison control center in your town. Record it here:

Poison Control Center: _____

Address _____

Phone Number _____

CHAPTER NINE

Know Your Soil and Fertilizer

For many years I felt embarrassed whenever I heard an energetic gardener use the lifeless term "dirt" in describing the miracle media that support plant life. "Soil" is such a nice word – why say dirt? Then came the ultimate. I met a delightfully enthusiastic gardener from Sweden who questioned me one afternoon over a drooping dracena plant, "Maybe I should change the *mud*?" Since that day I have not felt embarrassed when hearing the term "dirt" used for "potting soil."

Regardless of what you call it, remember *soils are alive* and this is the most important lesson you'll learn. Here then is the section you've been waiting for – the "dirty" section.

ALL ABOUT SOIL

Deep within the earth there is a hard rock called parent material. Earth movement causes this rock to break into smaller chunks called subsoil. The melting and drying, freezing and thawing, and action of roots and animals keep the upper portion of this layer broken into fine particles called surface soil. It is within this surface soil that plant roots seek nourishment and support. The larger particles in surface soil are called *sand* while the finer particles are called *clay*. The intermediate particles are called *silt*. If your soil has sufficient amount of organic matter mixed in, it is called *loam*. Loam is an excellent potting soil. When making your own potting soil, mix various portions of organic matter (*humus* from the compost pile or peat moss) with sand and you will have a sandy-loam soil, one of the best for growing Florida plants. A soil of this type will contain a sufficient proportion of air, water, organic matter, and minerals.

Air is necessary for healthy root growth and for prevention of root decay.

The only soil water that is available to plants is the moisture held between the soil particles. When all these tiny spaces are filled, the soil is said to be at field capacity. Any water added beyond this is superfluous and will run out the drain holes of the pot. A good potting soil will contain about 25% air and 25% water.

An average garden soil will contain about 5% organic matter, while a good potting soil may contain 25% organic matter, and in some cases 50%. Organic matter is humus or partially decomposed grass clippings, leaves, or other materials commonly thrown in a compost pile. Add extra nitrogen fertilizer to a soil mix that contains a large percentage of fresh or partially decomposed organic matter. The nitrogen is necessary to "feed" the decomposing bacteria. That brings us to an interesting point. A good garden soil is alive with little living things that help plants grow.

Soil Organisms

Organic gardeners are very much aware of these tiny fellows in their soil. The organic gardener's motto is "feed the soil; not the plant." He has learned that by creating a healthy environment for soil organisms (lots of organic matter, moisture, humus, heat, nitrogen, and aeration) he can ignore the plants. He feeds the soil; the soil feeds the plants.

1. Earthworms: The movement of earthworms creates excellent aeration for the soil. They may migrate to a depth of six feet to break up hardpan. Dead bodies of earthworms are themselves a rich boost. And their castings have a fertilizer analysis of 5-7-11, rich in nitrogen, phosphorus, and potash.

2. Nematodes: Certain species of these microscopic worms thrive on organic matter in the soil and help break it down to where the nutrients in the organic material become available to growing plants.

3. Protozoa: These one-celled animals maintain a balance of soil populations by feeding on certain bacteria.

4. Actinomycetes: Even smaller than protozoa, the actinomycetes are instrumental in decomposing organic matter making available bound nitrogen.

5. Fungi: Fungi rot plant tissue. This is harmful to plants but becomes an asset for dead plants and compost. Most fungi live below the surface in warm, damp soils.

6. Bacteria: Over three billion bacteria exist in a single gram of soil. They are extremely small, abundant and useful in garden soils. Some species convert ammonia to a usable form of nitrogen, while others absorb nitrogen from the air and convert it to a form useful to plants.

Soil organisms play a major role in keeping a soil in balance. They feed upon dead plants, animals, and manure, releasing natural fertilizers and CO_2 to our plants.

Minerals

Mineral elements make up the bulk of most natural soils. Minerals are such elements as iron, calcium, magnesium, and manganese. You will recognize these as fertilizers. Other names for minerals are elements, fertilizers, nutrients, and plant foods. The important subject of fertilizers is covered in the last half of this chapter.

Now that we have discussed a basic cross section of soils, let's look at some of the more practical applications in the study of soils.

Ten Facts About Florida Soils

1. The color of soil is no indication of its fertility or acidity. Often people believe black soil is good soil. Sometimes this is true, but often black soil is deficient in all nutrients except nitrogen.

2. Clay or muck soils should have coarse sand added to keep them from compacting. Many growers add 30% sawdust or wood chips to reduce compaction.

3. Hard-packed surface soils can be made more useful to the gardener by growing a cover crop of clover or soy beans and mulching heavily with grass clippings, sawdust, and stable manure. All of this should be rototilled into the soil at the end of the season before sodding.

4. Sand Soils can be made more productive by spreading a truckload of topsoil over the entire property and rototilling. Hand-pull any nutgrass that appears in a few weeks.

5. Hardpan is a hard, mineral stain layer in the soil that is often found a couple of feet under the surface. It inhibits root growth and is frequently detected when water stands for several hours on a lawn after a long rain. Eliminate this problem by digging deep drain holes every fifteen feet in the lawn or garden area. These holes, made with posthole diggers, should be filled with coarse gravel and topped with a good top soil. Be sure to dig one of these drain holes under every newly planted tree or large shrub. Pine trees will grow well on hardpan soils.

6. Peat soils are usually acidic and should have lime added to neutralize them before planting.

7. Dry spots in a lawn usually indicate one of several things: nematode damage (professional treatment required) or someone has buried concrete, plaster, boards, etc., just below the surface. Probe to determine if this is the problem. Occassionally, there is a depression in the clay subsoil that renders the above surface soil too well-drained, and the nutrients are being leached out. Top-dress by raking in a rich top soil every six months, and apply extra organic fertilizer to the area each season.

8. Soft, sandy soils that are too loose to support plant life sufficiently and are too well-drained to hold mositure can be rendered more useful by adding colloidal phosphate to stiffen it. Spread at a ratio of one or two pounds per 1,000 sq. ft.

9. Water table is the term used to indicate the surface depth of water *beneath* our soils. If you dig a four-foot hole and hit water, you have a four-foot water table at that time. Water tables change according to the rainy season. Little can be done if the water table comes up under your plants and they begin to die. If the plants are small enough, transplant them to a two-foot mound of top soil.

10. Black soils often disappear when digging just below the surface because of a distinct zone of leaching. During heavy rains, organic matter tends to float, increasing the dark color at the soil surface.

ALL ABOUT FERTILIZERS

Just as people have certain vitamin and mineral requirements to remain healthy, plants require at least seventeen fertilizer elements (legally called plant foods in Florida) to maintain good health. These are: carbon, hydrogen, and oxygen – available from air and water; nitrogen, phosphorus, and potash – available in fertilizers and called *primary plant foods;* and magnesium, copper, manganese, zinc, boron, iron, molybdenum, sulfur, and calcium–available in the soil, in spray residues, and added as *secondary plant foods* in fertilizers. Chlorine is also necessary, but is often abundant in soils and fertilizer fillers and may even become toxic if high concentrations are found in the soil. Aluminum has more recently been thought to be necessary for normal plant growth and is usually found in sufficient quantities in the soil. There are probably minute traces of other mineral elements necessary for healthy plants found in the soil, but they have not yet been identified. For this reason, I add a certain amount of garden soil to my homemade mixes

When buying fertilizer there are three things a good gardener will always look for: the N-P-K analysis, percentage of organic materials, and secondary plant foods.

N-P-K Analysis

N-P-K stands for the three elements required in the largest quantity by green plants: nitrogen (N), phosphorus (P), and potash (K). Analysis refers to the percentage of each of these elements found in a bag of fertilizer. For instance, 6-6-6 stands for 6% each of N, P, and K; 5-10-5 means the bag contains 5% nitrogen, 10% phosphorus, and 5% potash. If you are looking at a 50 lb. bag of 4-6-8, it contains 2 lbs. of nitrogen, 3 lbs. of phosphorus, and 4 lbs. of potash. Analysis is the percentage, not the actual number of pounds. In other words, 4% of 50 lbs. is 2 lbs. not 4 lbs.

A *complete fertilizer* contains some of each of these three elements. Fertilizers with an analysis like 6-4-0 or 20-0-0 are not complete and should be used as special fertilizers, not as a general purpose plant food.

In a bag of 6-6-6 there is a total of 18% (6 + 6 + 6) primary plant foods. What fills the remaining 82% of the bag? A filler is added to prevent the mineral elements from caking and to facilitate spreading. This filler is often dolomite, raw phosphate, sand, or sludge, and very often contains secondary plant foods such as magnesium and calcium.

Nitrogen is used abundantly in grasses and foliage house plants where lush, green, leafy growth is required. A high nitrogen fertilizer like 20-5-5 will make grasses a rich green color.

Phosphorus stimulates a heavy root system that gives a plant increased health and vigor. Fertilizers like 2-10-2 are used on young seedlings to help them develop a strong root system.

Potash has been called powdered sunshine because it adds strength and quality to fruits and flowers. Potash also helps build disease resistance in plants. Fertilizers like 4-6-8 contain a high percentage of potash and are used on fruiting trees such as citrus. A bloomer fertilizer for flowers has an analysis of 2-10-10. Many flowering plants such as geranium, nasturtium, and tomato will actually drop flower buds and flush out new leaves if given a high-nitrogen fertilizer.

- **NITROGEN** for lush green leaves
- **PHOSPHORUS** for a strong root system
- **POTASH** for flowers, fruit & disease resistance

Percent Organic

The second point of importance refers only to nitrogen – is it organic or inorganic? Nitrogen that comes from organic or living sources has certain characteristics that make it different from inorganic or chemical-source nitrogen. Here is a comparison of the two:

ORGANIC NITROGEN	INORGANIC NITROGEN
1. More costly	1. Less expensive
2. Less soluble so does not leach out in heavy rain	2. Dissolves readily so will wash away in heavy rain
3. A slow-release nitrogen	3. A rapid-feed nitrogen
4. Overdose does not burn	4. Overdose burns plants
5. Neutral in reaction	5. May acidify the soil
6. Contains secondary plant foods	6. Contains no secondary foods
7. Lasts 2 to 6 months	7. Lasts only 30 days
8. Less available to plants in cold weather	8. Available to plants year-round

Secondary Plant Foods

The third thing to determine when buying fertilizer is whether or not it contains any secondary plant foods such as iron, copper, or magnesium. A complete fertilizer with a well-balanced analysis, high percent organic, and several secondary plant foods will normally cost more but is the best for your plants. Often these fertilizers advertise their contents on the front label. If not, look at the contents label to determine these three factors. The most common secondary plant foods are magnesium and iron (both at 1% or more), manganese, copper, zinc, boron, and molybdenum (each in small traces).

How to Read a Fertilizer Label

Fertilizer labels are not hard to read and can save you money if you know how to read them. Let's look at a label from a typical palm special fertilizer and see what we can learn.

1. The N-P-K analysis is always the first three numbers in the right hand column. Here it is seen to be 6-6-6 and is called total nitrogen, available phosphoric acid, and water-soluble potash.

2. The percent organic is found in the subdivisions under *total nitrogen*. Nitrate nitrogen and ammoniacal nitrogen are inorganic forms. Water-soluble organic, urea, and water-insoluble nitrogen are all organic forms. Simply place in the numerator the total of the organic forms $(0.30 + 1.20 = 1.50)$. Place in the denominator the total nitrogen (6). Then convert this fraction to a percentage by dividing the denominator into the numerator, or 6 into 1.5. The answer is .25 or 25% organic.

It is important, however, to point out that while water-soluble organic and urea forms of nitrogen are actually organic, they will last only about

PALM SPECIAL
MINIMUM GUARANTEED ANALYSIS

Total Nitrogen		6.00%
Nitrate Nitrogen	0.75%	
Ammoniacal Nitrogen	3.75%	
Water-soluble Organic Nitrogen	0.30%	
(and/or Urea Nitrogen)	-------%	
Water-insoluble Nitrogen	1.20%	
Available Phosphoric Acid		6.00%
Water-soluble Potash		6.00%
Total Available Primary Plant Food		18.00%
Chlorine, not more than		6.00%

Primary Plant Food sources: Activated sludge, High-grade tankage, Sulphate of ammonia, Ammoniated superphosphate, Muriate of potash, Sul-Po-Mag.

Secondary Plant Foods

Total Magnesium as MgO	2.00 %	Copper as CuO	0.028%
W/S Magnesium as MgO	2.00 %	Zinc as ZnO	0.065%
Iron as Fe_2O_3	1.193%	Boron as B_2O_3	0.073%
Manganese as MnO	2.070%	Molybdenum as MoO_3	0.002%

Secondary Plant Food sources: Sul-Po-Mag, Iron sulphate, Manganese Oxide, Fritted trace elements.

---

thirty days in the soil. The water-insoluble nitrogen is the one that will last for six months or longer. This is the form of nitrogen found in natural organics such as cow manure, sludge, chicken manure, and tankage. In this palm special, after thirty days, only 20% ($1.2 \div 6$) of the fertilizer will be left in the soil for continued feeding. If you want a fertilizer that lasts longer than thirty days, buy one with a high percentage of water-insoluble nitrogen.

3. *The secondary elements* are seen at the bottom of the label and this palm special has lots of them: magnesium, iron, manganese, copper, zinc, boron, and molybdenum. Notice that the sources of both the primary and secondary plant foods are also given.

Our palm special label revels this mixture to be a 6-6-6 complete fertilizer, 25% organic with 20% slow feed, and containing several trace elements. While the manufacturer has called this a palm special (because of the high percentage of manganese palms demand) it would be a good general fertilizer for lawns, shrubs, and trees in the early spring when they need a boost.

How Much Fertilizer to Use

The amount of fertilizer to use on plants as recommended by the manufacturer is based on the percentage of nitrogen in the bag. If 6-6-6

FERTILIZER RATES

WHAT	HOW MUCH	WHEN
Annual Flower Beds	2 lbs./100 sq. ft.	February, June, October
Bulbs & Perennials	2 lbs./100 sq. ft.	February, June, October
Roses	1 cupful	each month during growing season
Shrubs	½ cup for 2-ft. spread 1 cup for 4-ft. spread	every 3 months
Trees & Palms	1 lb. for each 1 inch of trunk diameter	February, June, October
Fruit Trees	trees under 10 years get 1 lb. for each year of age; trees over 10 get ½ lb. for each year of age	February, June, October
Hedge Rows	3 lbs. for every 25 ft. of hedge	February, June, October
Lawn	25 lbs./1000 sq. ft.	February, June, October

is recommended to be applied at a rate of 25 lbs. per 1000 sq. ft. of lawn area, then 3-6-6 would be applied at 50 lbs. per 1000 sq. ft. In this respect, the lawn would receive the same amount of actual nitrogen but different quantities of phosphorus and potash.

Now, it can be seen why a 50-lb. bag of 6-6-6 will cover only 2000 sq. ft., while a 50-lb. bag of 25-5-5 will cover 8000 sq. ft. The 6-6-6 is applied at 25 lbs. per 1000 sq. ft.; the 25-5-5, being four times as strong in total nitrogen, is applied at only 6 lbs. per 1000 sq. ft. and will cover four times as much area. Both lawns will receive approximately the same amount of nitrogen, but the 25-5-5 lawn receives very small amounts of phosphorus and potash. A 25-5-5 fertilizer is good for greening the blades but will not give lawns the vigorous root system and disease-resistance they need. For this reason, a more balanced fertilizer, like 6-6-6, is recommended for lawns. An occasional application of 25-5-5 to green up color is permissible.

Special fertilizers will have the recommended rates printed on their labels. Examples of these types of fertilizers would be palm special, rose special, iron sulfate, bloomer, citrus special, manganeze sulfate (epsom salts), azalea special, Bahia special, etc. Each of these fertilizers have been slightly altered to better match specific plants' requirements. For the homeowner who wishes to keep his fertilizer closet as simple as possible, however, I recommend using 6 6 6, 50% to 100% organic, with all seven secondary elements. This fertilizer is the best all-round plant food for Florida lawns and gardens.

These fertilizers should be placed where they will be received *by the roots* of the plant being fertilized. If you have a large tree with deep roots, or a hedge or palm with grass growing around the base, be sure to plug holes in the sod one foot deep to get the fertilizer down where you want it.

Hunger Signs

If your plants become deficient in one or more plant foods, they will show tell-tale signs of this hunger. Usually these signs are centered around the leaves and their veins. Following are some typical hunger signs seen on Florida plants.

1. Nitrogen Deficiency: Entire leaf turns yellow (especially older leaves) and plants appear hungry and growth slows. Early stages are pale green leaves. Gardenia, hibiscus, citrus, and other broadleaf evergreens drop several yellow leaves each spring due to a normal shedding process. Don't confuse this with nitrogen deficiency.

2. Phosphorus Deficiency: Leaves and stems turn a purple shade especially on leaf margins (viburnum does this normally in the winter). There is general stunting and delayed fruiting.

3. Potash Deficiency Twigs decrease in size. Leaves may appear crinkled.

4. Calcium Deficiency: Immature leaves. Tip dieback occurs on limbs.

5. Magnesium Deficiency: Lower leaf vein remains green while outer leaf begins to yellow. Leaves may turn a bronze color. Often seen on citrus leaves. Look for a dark green inverted "V."

6. Sulfur Deficiency: Light leaves with lighter veins.

7. Molybdenum Deficiency: Causes leaf curl on lyches (called "strap

| PHOSPHORUS DEFICIENCY | MAGNESIUM DEFICIENCY | MANGANESE DEFICIENCY | IRON DEFICIENCY |

leaf''). Don't confuse with leaf curl on citrus and other plants caused by aphids. Look for the aphids. Leaves may develop yellow spots.

8. *Manganese Deficiency:* Similar to iron deficiency but green veins have a more ragged coloration. Common on allamanda, carissa, oaks, jasmine, and causes fronds of palms to turn yellow (called "frizzle top" on Cocos plumosa).

9. *Copper Deficiency:* Branches may take on an "S" shape, multiple budding, twig dieback.

10. *Zinc Deficiency:* Leaves appear smaller with some mottled, variegated appearance.

11. *Iron Deficiency:* Called iron chlorosis. Veins remain green while interveins begin to yellow. Common on gardenia. Also causes Bahia lawns to turn yellow in the spring.

12. *Boron Deficiency:* Leaves become wilted, curled, or puckered and take on a dull, brownish-green color.

Is Your Soil Sweet Or Sour?

The sweetness of your soil is related to plant food availability, as we will see in a moment. The Indians and early farmers in America noticed that soil with a slightly sour taste grew plants better than soil with a sweet taste. With today's technology we don't have to "bite the dust" to know if it will grow plants. What we are talking about is soil acidity. It is measured in pH which stands for potential hydrogen and technically is defined as the negative logarithm of the hydrogen ion concentration – but who wants to be technical?

The pH of a soil can be measured with a simple kit available on the market for a few dollars, complete with instructions. Similar kits are used to test swimming pools and fish aquariums.

The pH range is from 1 to 14. A soil with a pH of 7 is neutral. If pH is less than 7 the soil is acid (sour), if greater than 7 it is alkaline (sweet).

Most plants prefer a pH of 5 to 7, with 6 being ideal. The acid lovers

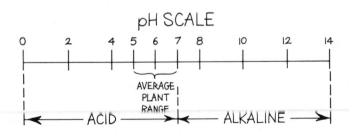

such as azalea, gardenia, hydrangea, and blackberries will grow best
when the pH is 4 or 5. Few plants grow in a soil with a pH over 7.
The acid soils (low pH), which are apt to be highly organic, are

DESIRABLE PH RANGES

Strongly Acid Below pH 5.4	Moderately to Strongly Acid pH 5.5-5.9	Moderately Acid pH 6.0-6.4	Slightly Acid pH 6.5-6.9
Woody Ornamentals			
Azalea	Allamanda	Allamanda	Arborvitae
Bougainvillea	Amer. redbud	Amer. redbud	Butterfly bush
Crape myrtle	Arborvitae	Arborvitae	Crape myrtle
Croton	Azalea	Bougainvillea	Croton
Feijoa	Bougainvillea	Butterfly bush	Feijoa
Firethorn	Camellia	Camellia	(also to pH 7.5)
Flowering dogwood	Citrus	Citrus	Firethorn
Gardenia	Crape myrtle	Crape myrtle	Pink hydrangea
Hibiscus	Croton	Croton	(also to pH 7.5)
Amer. holly	Feijoa	Feijoa	Oleander
Blue hydrangea	Firethorn	Firethorn	Palms
Ligustrum	Flowering dogwood	Flowering dogwood	Red cedar
Magnolia	Gardenia	Gardenia	Sycamore
Oleander	Glossy abelia	Glossy abelia	Yucca
Pittosporum	Hibiscus	Hibiscus	
Podocarpus	Amer. holly	Ligustrum	
Yaupon	Ligustrum	Magnolia	
	Magnolia	Oleander	
	Oleander	Palms	
	Palms	Pittosporum	
	Pittosporum	Podocarpus	
	Podocarpus	Red cedar	
	Shrimp plant	Shrimp plant	
	Wisteria	Sycamore	
	Yaupon	Wisteria	
		Yaupon	
		Yucca	
Garden Flowers			
Blue lupine	Amaryllis	Amaryllis	Begonia
China aster	Begonia	Begonia	Carnation
Coreopsis	Blue lupine	Calendula	China aster
Pansy	Calendula	Carnation	Day lily
Phlox	China aster	China aster	Marigold
	Chrysanthemum	Chrysanthemum	Nasturium
	Coreopsis	Day lily	Petunia
	Gladiolus	Gladiolus	Poinsettia
	Lycoris	Easter lily	Rose
	Marigold	Lycoris	Snapdragon
	Morea	Marigold	Zinnia
	Narcissus	Morea	
	Nasturtium	Narcissus	
	Pansy	Nasturtium	
	Petunia	Pansy	
	Phlox	Petunia	
	Rose	Poinsettia	
	Snapdragon	Rose	
	Zinnia	Snapdragon	
		Zinnia	

those containing large amounts of decaying organic matter, muck, or peat, and those found around oak trees. In these cases the pH is usually 3 or 4 and will need to be increased.

The alkaline soils (high pH) are those that contain large quantities of limestone. Foundation beds around homes often have buried in them limestone-containing mortar, plaster, cement, or other building materials. Those lands that were filled from bay bottom dredging contain large quantities of shell. In these cases the pH will be around 8 and will require an additive to reduce the pH.

To increase soil pH one point, add 65 lbs. of dolomite to each 1000 sq. ft. of soil surface. Repeat every 30 days, raising pH one point each month, until desired pH is attained.

To decrease the soil pH one-half point, add 10 lbs. of wettable sulfur to every 1000 sq. ft. of soil surface (1 lb./100 sq. ft.). Never add more than 10 lbs. in any single application, otherwise plants may burn. Repeat your application every 30 days until the desired pH is attained.

Now, for the important question. *Why is a low or high pH bad for plant growth?* This question is best answered by looking at the plant food availability chart. The width of bar indicates relative availability of plant food.

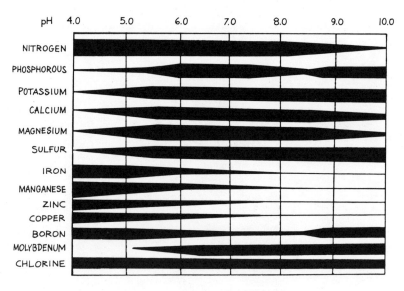

PLANT FOOD AVAILABILITY CHART

It can be seen that when the soil pH goes below 4, certain plant foods (fertilizer elements) in the soil become "locked up." Phosphorus, potash, calcium, magnesium, sulfur, and molybdenum are no longer available to the plant. This means if you are growing plants in a muck soil with a pH of 3 and you fertilize these plants, the fertilizers will quickly "lock up" and become unavailable to the plants. Plants then begin to show hunger signs. The solution is not to feed these hungry plants more fertilizer but to test the soil pH and add the necessary dolomite to raise the pH to 6, where the plant foods will be released back to the plants.

Likewise, when the pH goes above 7, iron, manganese, zinc, copper, and boron become locked. The solution is to test the pH and add the necessary amount of sulfur to reduce the pH to 6 where all plant foods are available.

Usually a soil amendment to adjust the pH is not a permanent adjustment. Periodic testing will reveal necessary action required.

Understanding soils and fertilizers is a must to gardeners who want to have success in growing plants and lawns. Florida soils are different. Often they are too well-drained or too poorly drained – seldom are they ideally drained. Often they are too acid or too alkaline. Reread this chapter from time to time. There are many helpful hints in it that will keep your thumb green.

CHAPTER TEN

Citrus, Tropical, Hardy, and Berry Fruits

I love fruit! I often recall in my youth swinging from limbs of mulberry trees, gulping down figs from our backyard garden, picking wild blackberries along a woodsy trail, or burrowing my face into a freshly picked and broken pomegranate, swallowing the rich juice and spitting forth a machine-gun spray of seeds. The fruit products are just as memorable – homemade preserves and jams, fruit salads, peach jacks, pies, and even ice cream. The climate in Florida is so conducive to fruit production that most of the hardier, northern fruits are grown here as are many tropicals. It's a fruit lover's paradise.

This chapter is presented in four major sections for easy reference: citrus fruits (oranges, grapefruits, etc.), tropical fruits (bananas, pineapples, etc.), hardy fruits (apples, figs, etc.), and the berry fruits (grapes, strawberries, etc.)

ORANGES AND OTHER CITRUS

Oranges belong to a rather large and popular group called citrus. Besides oranges, there are mandarins (a loose-skin class of which tangerines are a member), tangelos (a cross between a mandarin and a grapefruit, resembling an orange), grapefruits, and the acid members including lemons and limes.

Oranges and other citrus require a full twelve months to mature instead of the five- or six-month growing time of other fruits. When you travel through Florida, you may see both blossoms and fully ripened fruit on the same trees.

Another unusual characteristic of citrus is that the fruits require a minimum of 300 days of sunshine. Thus, Florida is one of the few places in the world where they can be grown successfully.

All citrus fruits are ripened by nature and must be fully mature at the time they are picked. The citrus industry had its beginning in Florida about 1579 near St. Augustine. Wherever the Spanish settled, citrus plantings soon appeared. Indians spread the seeds throughout the state, and by the 1800s citrus was being shipped north commercially. Today, Florida produces over 80% of the oranges, 50% of the grapefruits, and practically all of the tangelos, limes, and tangerines in the United States.

Seven Popular Oranges

1. Hamlin: Medium small fruit, nearly seedless, thin rind with finely pitted surface, well-colored, popular for juicing, good Christmas orange.

2. Parson Brown: Medium large fruit, moderately seedy, medium thin rind with finely pitted surface, dull color, firm, good for juice, well flavored, large vigorous tree, one of the earliest to mature in the fall, excellent quality.

3. Navel: Seedless, easy to peel and separate, rich in flavor, a popular orange for hand-eating, a very large fruit maturing in November or December, yields are not abundant, contains a navel-like structure on the bottom of the fruit.

4. Pineapple Orange: Excellent quality for juice or hand-eating, moderately seedy, medium large fruit, well-colored, medium thick rind with finely pitted surface, light orange inside, tender, juicy, sweet flavor; matures January-March, highly productive, but may be tender to frost.

5. Queen Similar to pineapple but slightly richer in flavor, less seedy, and holds better on tree.

6. Temple: Actually a tangor, a medium size fruit containing a few seeds, moderately juicy, rich flavor, deep color, a very popular hand-eating orange, thorny tree, good pollinator; matures around February; tree may be damaged by frost

7. Valencia: Medium large fruit, nearly seedless, tough rind with faintly pebbled surface, the most popular juice orange; holds exceptionally well on tree; last orange to mature, usually after April; large prolific tree with alternate bearing tendencies that cause it to bear heavily one year and lightly the next. Lue Gim Gong is a Valencia variety.

Seven Popular Mandarins

Often called loose-skin oranges, the mandarins have fruit smaller than oranges with a compressed shape and an open core. The trees are slightly more cold sensitive.

1. Satsuma: Medium size, tangerine-type fruit, seedless, naval frequently present; thin, leathery rind; fruit drops after maturing in October-November, matures before turning orange; tree is small, slow-growing, nearly thornless, spreading and drooping; the hardiest of all citrus, it is resistant to temperatures as low as 15 degrees.

2. King: Large, tangerine-type; thick rind peals easily; seedy, tender, flavor; delicious eating; matures around March.

3. Dancy Tangerine: Medium size fruit with thin, tough, loose rind, moderately high in acid, moderately juicy, rich flavor, few seeds, popular for hand-eating, most important mandarin variety; matures around first of year; has slight alternate bearing tendencies; requires the heat and humidity found only in Florida.

4. Murcott Honey: Similar to Dancy tangerine in appearance and taste: matures February-March; very juicy, rich in flavor, peels easily; sensitive to cold, has alternate bearing tendencies – a nice looking gift fruit.

5. Robinson Tangerine: Medium large fruit, easily peeled, juicy, flavorful and sweet, moderately seedy; matures September-October, bears regularly.

6. Lee Tangerine: Medium size fruit; thin, leathery rind has smooth, glossy surface; abundant juice, rich and sweet.

7. Osceola Tangerine: A relatively new USDA hybrid that appears to be an excellent loose-skin tangerine; matures around November.

Five Popular Tangelos

Tangelos are a hybrid cross between a sweet mandarin and a tart grapefruit. They much resemble oranges with strong color, but are easier to peel and section. Tangelos have a luscious, invigorating flavor. Most trees bear heavier if cross-pollinated with temple orange.

1. Minneola: Large fruit with few seeds, medium thin rind, tender, juicy, aromatic; matures around first of year; has unusual exotic flavor.

2. Orlando: A popular tangelo, medium large with few seeds, tight thin rind, very juicy: cross-pollination recommended with dancy tangerine or temple orange; matures November-December, good yield.

3. Seminole: Medium large fruit, seedy, only slight adherence of thin rind, tender, juicy, tart flavor; resembles Minneola but peels easier and matures later.

4. Nova: Medium large fruit similar to Orlando tangelo; thin, leathery, loose rind, very sweet and juicy for hand-eating, deep orange color, 10-15 seeds; a strong, hardy tree, matures October-November.

5. Page: Medium size fruit, easily peeled, sweet, juicy flavor, deep orange color, good for hand-eating, 8-20 seeds. Looks much like a small orange. Matures November-December.

Five Popular Grapefruits

Most homeowners choose grapefruit varieties for their seedless character. Usually, the distinct quality that keeps a seedy variety on the market is the rich, succulent flavor that is unmatched by the seedless varieties.

1. Duncan: Large, seedy fruit, tender, very juicy, maturing from November-January; the standard of grapefruit excellence. Developed around 1830 in Safety Harbor, Florida; very popular, easily separated segments.

2. Marsh Seedless: Medium fruit with few seeds and thin, tough, smooth surface, very juicy but not quite as flavorful as the seedy varieties; matures late – from December-April; the leading white variety.

3. Thompson Pink Seedless: Medium size fruit, very smooth but tough rind, tender, juicy; holds well on tree, matures from November-January; pink-colored flesh, not as popular as Ruby Red.

4. Ruby Red Seedless: Sometimes called Red Marsh or Redblush; similar to Thompson but flesh is a much deeper red.

5. Foster Pink: A large, seedy, red-flesh fruit with smooth surface. The first pink grapefruit in Florida, it declined in popularity when replaced by Thompson pink seedless.

Nine Popular Acid Citrus Fruits

This group is prized for its tart, acid flavor so popular in salads, pies, drinks, and as a food seasoning. Try some of the alternates the next time you reach for a bottle of reconstituted lemon juice.

1. Ponderosa Lemon: Huge, yellow, seedy fruit (looks like an oval grapefruit) with thick, bumpy rind used in candying, a good pie lemon; may be damaged by frost, often bears year-round.

2. Meyer Lemon: Very juicy with thin, soft, smooth-surfaced rind, a few seeds; excellent lemon for kitchen use; more cold-hardy than other lemons, matures December-April, but bears some fruit year-round.

3. Bearss Lemon: Few to no seeds, looks and tastes like California lemon, matures in fall and winter.

4. Key Lime: Very small fruit; moderately seedy, very thin rind; drops from tree at maturity; tender, juicy, highly acid; used in popular Key lime pie and summer drinks; grows true from seed; sensitive to cold; semi-everbearing.

5. Tahiti Lime: Also called Persian lime: large fruit, usually no seeds, thin rind, juicy lime flavor; often bears year-round; sensitive to cold.

6. Bearss Lime: Practically identical to Tahiti lime.

7. Lakeland Limequat: An excellent lime substitute and a popular potted ornamental; cold-hardiness is better than most limes, bears mostly year-round; slightly seedy fruit is larger than lime.

8. Calamondin: Sold as the popular potted mini-orange, since small trees bear an abundance of fruit resembling little oranges. Fruit is size of lime, color of orange, and tastes like lemon; very hardy, bears fruit mostly fall through spring; used as a lemon-lime substitute.

9. Kumquat: *Nagami* variety is a very acid, oval-shaped fruit the size of a lime, used mostly for making marmalades and preserves. *Meiwa* variety is round and has a sweet flavor; can be peeled and eaten like an orange. Both varieties have few seeds and bear heavily from October-January.

HOW TO PLANT AND CARE FOR CITRUS

Citrus growing on home grounds is restricted to Central and Southern Florida, except for hardy varieties which thrive in protected locations of Northern Florida.

Trees bought from nurseries should be planted in a sandy, well-drained location and at the same depth as they were growing in the container. Never mulch the ground around citrus or allow grass or other ground covers to grow next to their trunks as this aids a disease called "foot rot."

If the planting site has bad drainage, prepare a raised planting bed six feet in diameter and at least one foot high. One yard of sandy topsoil is sufficient for this mound.

Most all Florida citrus trees are grafted or budded (see ch. 5) onto rootstocks of sour orange or trifoliate orange. Rough lemon rootstock is not used much anymore because of disease. When buying trees be sure they are budded or grafted. Lemons and limes do well without this graft. Seedling trees (those grown from seeds) take many years to bear. Occasionally a vigorous looking limb will grow from below the grafted area (a few inches above the ground). This limb is a *sucker* from the rootstock and should be cut off.

After an extended, heavy rain your tree may send out a long shoot with large leaves. These are called *water sprouts* and will bear fruit. But to keep the tree well shaped, cut off about half of this shoot.

Citrus plantings should be in full sun and spaced 25 feet apart. Satsuma, kumquat, calamondin, lemon, and lime trees require only 15 feet for growing.

Always avoid acid soil (see ch. 9), poor drainage, septic tanks and their drain fields. Tree roots will clog the drainage, and detergents, soaps, alkalies, borax, and other chemicals used in the home may injure the tree. Most citrus trees will grow about one foot in height and spread each year.

Trees grown in containers may be planted anytime of the year. If your tree is to be transplanted as either bare-root or balled-and-burlapped, it should be done in late January while still dormant. The next best time would be late spring after the first flush of growth and flowers.

Potted trees bought from nurseries are reasonably priced and are three years old. Often the fruit is picked off to allow more leaf growth for the future. If you plant one of these trees, water it twice a week, provided the tree receives no rain. Trees three years old or older should be fertilized three times a year, February, June, and October. Apply a citrus special fertilizer at one pound for each year of the tree's age up to ten years. An eight-year-old tree gets eight pounds each of the three months.

By the fourth or fifth year, your tree should be bearing good quality fruit. For trees over ten years old, apply just one-half pound of fertilizer for each year of age. To insure healthier trees, spray foliage of fruit-bearing trees with a nutritional spray once a year in the early spring. These sprays are available from garden supply stores.

Pruning of older trees is usually confined to removing dead or damaged limbs (see ch. 6). Prune only enough growth out of the center of the tree to facilitate fruit picking and spraying.

Trees that have been damaged by cold should not be pruned until the following spring. This delay allows the tree to recover from shock and for you to ascertain the degree of damage.

It is best to keep sprinkler systems away from citrus plantings as they do not like wet feet.

To protect trees from frost or cold, cover with a sheet or thin blanket on cold nights and burn three or four 100-watt lights under this tent. These bulbs will serve as heaters.

Because citrus trees are fruit bearers and a little on the tender side, they require more maintenance than shade trees. To prevent problems from occurring look over the following list of common ailments.

Twelve Problems Affecting Citrus

1. Sooty Mold: A black soot appears on the surface of most citrus leaves in the late summer and fall. It is caused by a fungus living on the

SOOTY
MOLD

WHITE FLY
AND EGGS

honeydew droppings of sucking insects. A soapy solution or oil spray will remove the soot. Oil sprays should not be used in temperatures over 90 degrees. The best control is to wait until the weather cools in early fall and spray malathion and oil or ethion and oil to control both insects and fungus.

2. Aphids: In the early spring during blossom season, these sucking insects feed on the underside of the leaves causing them to curl. Spray malathion every week just before blooms open, and again just after they fall.

3. White Fly: Tiny, white specks will be seen flying around leaves during the warm months; or look for tan, rounded flakes about the size of a pin head on the underside of leaves. This sucking insect, as well as all scales, aphids, and mealy-bugs are kept under control by spraying malathion every two weeks or ethion every sixty days during the growing season (see ch. 1, Sucking Insects).

There are several fungi that feed upon white fly larvae and usually appear as bright orange or yellow bumps under the leaves. This friendly fungus is beneficial and requires no control.

4. Decline Diseases: This title is a catch-all term that refers to a number of diseases or environmental problems that obstruct the movement of water and nutrients through the plant. They frequently cause the root system to decay. Symptoms include general thinning and foliage loss, and the dying back of twigs and small limbs. There is often a reduction in fruit quantity and size. Usually all the homeowner can do is prune back severely (see ch. 6) and keep the tree as healthy as possible through proper watering, feeding, and spraying.

5. Magnesium Deficiency: Caused by improper fertilizing; can be corrected by applying magnesium sulfate (epsom salts) at five pounds to half-grown trees and fifteen pounds to fully grown trees. Symptoms appear as yellowing leaves with the main vein remaining green. This green area widens at the base of the vein near the stem.

6. Fruit Split: Each year during the late summer rainy season, numerous cases of splitting fruit are reported. This malady is caused by the tree absorbing considerable amounts of moisture and forcing it into the fruit. Since the fruit is nearly mature at this stage, the rind is less pliable, does not expand rapidly to accommodate the excess moisture, and splits. Water trees heavily during drought seasons, and always use a trace-element fertilizer. This will help prevent the rind from toughening prematurely.

7. Rust Mites: These tiny creatures cause one side of the fruit to turn a rusty brown. Spray entire tree with Kelthane or sulfur to prevent these and other mites from weakening growth. (see ch. 1, Miscellaneous Insects.)

8. Brown Spots on Leaves or Fruit: Several fungus diseases may cause numerous brown or tan colored scabs or bumps on surface of leaves or fruit. Melanose, greasy spot, scab, anthracnose, algal spores, and pitting are a few. Neutral copper sprays applied every two to four weeks beginning one week after fruit is set, should eliminate these diseases. If control measures are not taken, leaves will yellow and fall, and the tree will go into a slow decline.

9. Leaf Drop: This condition could be any of a number of things, but on most home grounds it is caused by overwatering or poor drainage. Leaves usually turn yellow, then fall. Transplant shock could cause the same symptoms. Look for yellow veins that precede leaf drop.

10. Orange Dog Caterpillar: Two or three of these prolific chewers may completely devour the foliage from a young tree in just a few days. They are brown and gray mottled with an enlarged head that sends up what appears to be an orange forked snake tongue when disturbed. They do not sting and are controlled by dusting or spraying Sevin, or by stepping on the larger ones.

ORANGE DOG
CATERPILLAR

FOOT ROT

11. Foot Rot: This fungus disease affects the trunk usually just above the bud area. Bark begins to slough off, and drops of gum appear. Twigs may start to die back, fruit appears small, leaves lose their color, and the tree begins a slow decline. Foot rot is caused by mulching or allowing weeds or grass to grow at the base of the trunk. Damaging the base of the tree with a shovel when planting it or bumping it with a lawn mower has also caused this problem. Control is to cut away all diseased wood and spray area with neutral copper, then paint exposed wood with black pruning paint.

12. Fruit Fly: Many fruit flies exist that lay eggs under the skin of the fruit. Eggs hatch into white worms that burrow into the fruit making it unfit for human consumption. Control is difficult, and includes gathering and destroying all fruit, and drenching the ground with diazinon to destroy the tiny worms. This practice usually eliminates a repeated infestation the following year.

TROPICAL FRUITS OF FLORIDA

Tropical fruits can be grown in frost-free locations of Florida or in protected areas of the northern part of the state. Even in frost areas, damage is usually slight, and plants recover rapidly. So, don't be afraid to try the tropicals. Besides cold-protection, most tropical fruits require good drainage and fertilization twice a year. Little pruning is required.

Want to grow your own plants? Most of the fruits produce viable seed and can be propagated by this means. But, since many of the young seedlings often differ from the mother plant, it would be wiser to use the seedling as a rootstock and graft or bud a portion of the mother plant onto it. The simplest solution, of course, is to buy grafted trees from a local nursery. Most nurseries won't carry a full line of fruit trees, but each county usually has at least one nurseryman specializing in tropical fruits. Get on the phone and call around until you find him.

Untold rewards are in store for the Florida homeowner who takes advantage of the wise selection of fruits available for his consumption. Not only can most of these trees provide fresh fruit for hand-eating, but there is always enough extra on hand for preserves, pickles, jellies, jams, and for freezing. Many cookbooks written for Florida will give you delicious recipes.

Ten Tropical Fruits

1. Banana (*Musa,* spp.): You can grow your own bananas by digging up young plants growing in a clump. Be sure to give them plenty of water and mulch heavily. They will grow fast and produce large, green leaves year-round if protected from frost and fed often. It takes about one year for the new plant to reach maturity and produce fruit. Cut the fruit stalks from the clumps as they begin to yellow.

2. Pineapple *(Ananas comosus):* Pineapple is an interesting exotic that is easy to grow, but sometimes difficult to get to bear fruit. Some growers drop a pinch of calcium carbide in the center of the plant while others place an apple (which gives off ethylene gas) under a sheet of clear polyethylene with the pineapple. As the new pineapple matures on a ¼-inch stalk, the old plant dies. Pineapple plants do not like a draft, salt air, excess water, or limestone soils.

3. Papaya *(Carica papaya):* Papayas come in male, female, and bisexual. The female is the only one that bears a heavy crop of fruit, but a male tree must be planted near the female to get cross-pollination. Grown from seed, young trees should be set in a rich, well-drained soil. They grow fast and bear in about twelve months. Most trees die in five or six years. Fruit may require covering with clear polyethylene to prevent insects from stinging it.

4. Coconut *(Cocos nucifera):* A long-time favorite, the coconut grows atop a tall palm tree. Residents of South Florida know the tree well; but the cold weather often kills it in Central and North Florida. The tree bears year-round and the fruit can be eaten both green and ripe.

5. Lychee *(Litchee chinensis):* The lychee has fruit much like a grape under its tough, red, bumpy skin – not too sour, not too sweet. The golf-ball size fruit is often borne in attractive clusters weighing up to 20 lbs. The trees are very well-shaped and grow in Central and South Florida as a shade tree.

PINEAPPLE   LYCHEE   CARAMBOLA

6. Carambola *(Averrhoa carambola):* This 20-foot upright tree will withstand temperatures as low as 20 degrees. The fruit is light yellow with a shiny waxed appearance. It resembles a three-inch football in shape, but has five deep creases down its sides giving a cut slice a star shape. Many carambolas are quite acid and used only for jellies, but some are sweet and eaten out of the hand

7. Feijoa *(Feijoa sellowiana)* The fruit is oval, about two or three inches long, and a dull green. Under the thin skin is thick white flesh that encloses a translucent jelly-like pulp embedded with 20 or 30 seeds. The flavor is similar to pineapple and strawberry. The plant makes a compact shrub up to fifteen feet and grows throughout Florida. The fruit is eaten fresh, stewed, or made into jam or jelly. Pick only when fully ripened.

8. Sapodilla *(Achras zapota):* This large, brown, sweet fruit matures from February to June. Sapodilla can be eaten fresh, frozen, or in sherbets. The medium size trees keep their leaves year-round and make fine wind barriers with a moderate resistance to salt air. They are also good shade trees for a small lot.

9. Mango *(Mangifera indica):* This "apple of the tropics" is one of Central and South Florida's most desirable shade trees. It looks especially nice around Spanish-style homes. The fruit, a kin to poison ivy, may cause an allergic reaction in susceptible eaters. But to most, it is quite desirable eaten fresh, in salads, or made into custards or ice cream. The trees prefer a rich, well-drained soil and plenty of fertilizer until they start to bear.

10. Guava *(Psidium* spp.*):* Of the many guava species, the two most often grown in Florida are Cattley guava *(Psidium cattleianum)* and common guava *(Psidium guajava).* Growing to two inches across, the round cattleya comes in several different varieties depending upon color. High in vitamin C (especially the skin), Cattley guavas vary in flavor from sweet (red) to acid (yellow), and are eaten fresh or preserved. "Florida's peach," the pear-shaped, yellow-skinned common guava, grows to six inches, with flesh ranging from white to reddish-pink. Also high in vitamin C, this versatile fruit is hand-eaten, canned, juiced; made into jelly, butter, sherbert, and pies. Propagated by seed, air layers, or grafts, both trees produce much fruit. Provide good drainage for trees and fertilize in March and June with 50% organic 6-6-6. Water well during fruit production.

HARDY FRUITS OF FLORIDA

Besides the tropicals, there are numerous hardier fruits that are more common to the northern and central part of the state. Many of these, though, will still thrive and produce in warmer South Florida areas. Look around your neighborhood or ask a neighbor (he probably just moved down from Ohio) if he knows of any such trees growing in your area. Or better yet, call your County Extension Director.

Ten Hardy Fruits

1. Mulberry *(Morus* spp.): A well-shaped shade tree that drops its leaves in winter, the mulberry is a fast grower that takes much cold and drought. The berries resemble blackberries and stain your clothing or driveway, but are quite palatable. They are eaten fresh or in pies and preserves. Seeds often produce inferior trees. Cuttings or grafting is better.

2. Pomegranate *(Punica granatum):* One of the oldest shrubs known to man, the fruit of the pomegranate is the size of an orange; has a red to yellow skin that when peeled reveals hundreds of tiny seeds covered with delicious, juicy red flesh. To eat just bite into the peeled fruit and spit out the seeds. Use the seeds to garnish salads, or squeeze to make juice or pudding sauce.

3. Fig *(Ficus carica):* The fig is one of the oldest known laxatives. The fruit is soft and eaten skin and all. The tree grows to about twelve feet and should be sprayed with ferbam or copper to help control fig rust, a disease causing small brown spots on leaves. Plants are often grown from two-foot cuttings made in the winter. Excellent varieties for Florida are Brown Turkey and Celeste.

4. Persimmon *(Diospyros kaki):* The oriental persimmon fruit produced on twelve-foot trees is a Florida favorite and is rich in food value, especially dextrose. Trees are bare in the winter and will usually require cross-pollination for fruit to appear.

5. Loquat *(Eriobotrya japonica):* A handsome broadleaf evergreen, this tree produces delicious yellow-orange fruit that is eaten skin and all or made into jam. Fertilize in March and June, but not too heavily. These trees make excellent small shade trees in the corner of a sunny garden. Better known varieties are Advance, Premier, and Gold Nugget.

6. Avocado *(Persea americana):* Depending on variety, the fruit may

POMEGRANATE   LOQUAT   AVOCADO

be green, black, purple, or reddish. Allow fruit to fall at maturity. Trees grow easily from seed, but should be grafted to produce superior fruit. Plant in well-drained locations and spray with neutral copper every thirty days beginning in February to prevent fungus diseases. The avocado is often called "Florida pear" or "alligator pear." Because of the pollination problem, it would be wise to plant two different varieties; one a morning-bloomer such as Taylor or Lulu, the other an afternoon-bloomer such as Hall.

7. Plum *(Prunus salicinas):* As with most fruits, plums like a sandy, well-drained soil. This small tree has an attractive appearance and is often planted solely for its ornamental value – the fruit being a bonus. Cross-pollination is frequently necessary, so plant two or three different varieties in a grouping. If one of these is the native Florida wild plum, it will be an excellent pollinator. A mixture of captan and Volck oil sprayed every two to four weeks while fruit is maturing will eliminate most problems. Good Central Florida varieties are Abundance and Excelsior, North Florida has numerous varieties.

8. Pear *(Pyrus serotina):* Pear is an excellent ornamental as well as fruitbearing tree. Fertilize and spray as for plums. Florida varieties include: Baldwin, Carnes, Hood, Kieffer, Le Conte, Orient, and Pineapple.

9. Apple *(Malus* spp.): Sure, we have apples in Florida. At least two varieties that I know of do well. One is Anna, a sweet red variety. The other is Ein Shemer. Both should be grafted and planted on a high, sunny location. Prune young trees to head them up. Fertilize in spring and summer.

10. Peach *(Amygdalus persica):* A real treat for hand-eating, canning, freezing, preserving; and for making jellies and jams. Only grafted varieties should be bought. One of the best for the warmer portions of the state is Flordawon. See your local nurseryman for varieties recommended to your area. Spray captan in the early spring and a mild solution of Volck oil during the summer for protection. Don't spray copper on peaches.

BERRY FRUITS OF FLORIDA

Florida also has many berry plants, often called small fruits, that are popular with gardeners. Several of these berries grow on vines that require a trellis. Others grow as small plants or large shrubs. Most of these berry fruits grow throughout the state.

If you can't find the plant you're looking for, contact one of the Agricultural Experimental Stations dotted throughout Florida for sources and newer variety names.

Eight Popular Berry Fruits

1. Grapes *(Vitis vinifera):* Everyone loves a good grape, and they can be grown almost anywhere in Florida. Grapes like a rich, sandy soil, well-mulched to keep out weeds. Plant container-bought plants ten feet apart on a three-wire trellis. Berries are produced only on wood grown the current season, so each December prune the vines back to six eyes on the previous season's growth. Fertilize in February with one to three pounds of 6-6-6 organic per plant. Malathion and captan will usually keep down the insects and diseases. Lake Emerald, Stover, Blue Lake, and Tamiami are good bunch grapes. Numerous muscadine varieties exist; many require pollinator plants. Try Higgins, Fry, and a Cowart to pollinate them.

2. Blueberries *(Vaccinium* spp.): Blueberries grow best in cooler portions of the state and where the soil is porous and acid. To maintain an acid level of pH-5 apply a little wettable sulfur every time you fertilize. The summer rainy season is the best time to plant blueberries bought in containers. Space plants ten feet apart and prevent weeds from growing under their many shoots by applying a heavy mulch of leaves, hay, or straw. Plant at least two different varieties to assure pollination. Blueberry culture is much like that of azalea. Titblue, Woodard, and Bluegem varieties are good for the warmer portions of the state.

3. Blackberries *(Rubus* spp.): Several varieties are native to Florida, but do not produce as well as Flordagrand, Brazos, and Oklawaha. Oklawaha serves as a good pollinator. Space plants six feet apart on a treated post or three-wire trellis. Apply one-half pound of a complete fertilizer to each plant every three months and spray with malathion as needed to control mites and thrips. Plants produce well if cut to the ground each year after the harvest.

4. Chinese Gooseberry *(Actinidia chinensis):* A fast-growing vine, it produces golf-ball size fruit that is brown and hairy on the outside, and sweet and green on the inside. Eat out of the hand or use in preserves. The Chinese gooseberry has good cold and drought resistance, but does not like wet feet. Try these varieties: Abbott, Allison, Bruno, Hayward. None are vigorous in South Florida.

5. Surinam Cherry *(Eugenia uniflora):* Surinam cherry is a rapidly growing barrier shrub often used as a hedge. New leaves have a reddish appearance. The abundant fruit is larger than an average cherry with grooves along the sides. Taste is sweet to tart. Eat fresh or make sherbet. If not pruned, plants will grow almost fifteen feet tall and nearly as wide. Maintenance is as for other landscape shrubs.

6. Strawberry *(Fragaria* spp.): About the only berry plant of commercial value in Florida is strawberry. Plants can be grown in many soil types but prefer soil high in organic matter which provides nourishment and water-holding capacity. However, good drainage is also important. In Central Florida (where strawberries are grown for commercial markets) plants are out around October, in September in North Florida, and in November in South Florida. Be sure the bud and crown are left entirely above ground with all roots in the ground. Fertilize at planting time and again one month later with a low nitrogen fertilizer such as a bloomer type. Strawberries like potash.

7. Barbados Cherry *(Malpighia glabra):* Also called malpighia, Barbados cherry makes an evergreen shrub. The large red cherries are juicy and sweet to tart in flavor. Eat fresh or use for juice. The fruits are high in vitamin C. Plant on a well-drained mound and fertilize with citrus special fertilizer.

8. Raspberry *(Rubus* spp.): A great jam fruit. The variety recommended for the warm portions of the state is Mysore, a black raspberry. Northern varieties do not grow in cool areas of Florida. Plant six feet apart on hills and tie canes to eight-foot stakes. As with most berry plants, roots are shallow, so cultivate weeds carefully. Water heavily and often. Fertilize with a low nitrogen (bloomer) fertilizer every month. Apply two handfuls (1/2 lb.) each time. Few insects or diseases bother the raspberry. Prune in late spring, summer, and fall to encourage lateral branching.

Index